Yes, My Accent Is Real

'Although I have never met this Kunal Nayyar fellow, I am told we have much in common. His little book is an intermittently entertaining read, although his understanding of basic physics (and of the proper way to woo a woman) is shockingly poor'

Raj Koothrappali, astrophysicist and star of
The Big Bang Theory

'Kunal Nayyar is a cultural icon in the United Kingdom. Then he wrote a book about India. He is therefore banished from the palace. Isn't it cool I live in a palace?'

The Queen of England

'I love this book so much!! It taught me that Kunal Nayyar is as weird as he looks and sounds ♥ #IKnowWhereYouLiveKunal'

Thirteen-Year-Old Fangirl

Kunal Nayyar was born in London and raised in New Delhi, India. He first came to the United States in 1999 to pursue a bachelor's degree in business administration and went on to receive an MFA in acting from Temple University. Playing the character of Raj on *The Big Bang Theory*, he has been part of the ensemble since the show debuted in 2007. He lives in Los Angeles with his wife, Neha.

Yes, My Accent Is Real

And Some Other Things
I Haven't Told You

❖

KUNAL NAYYAR

**SIMON &
SCHUSTER**

London · New York · Sydney · Toronto · New Delhi

A CBS COMPANY

First published in Great Britain by Simon & Schuster UK Ltd, 2015
A CBS COMPANY

1 3 5 7 9 10 8 6 4 2

Simon & Schuster UK Ltd
1st Floor
222 Gray's Inn Road
London WC1X 8HB

www.simonandschuster.co.uk

Simon & Schuster Australia, Sydney
Simon & Schuster India, New Delhi

A CIP catalogue record for this book
is available from the British Library

ISBN: 978-1-47115-278-8
ISBN: 978-1-47115-279-5 (Trade Paperback)
ISBN: 978-1-47115-561-1 (Trade Paperback India Edition)
ISBN: 978-1-47115-281-8 (ebook)

Interior design by Paul Dippolito
Printed and bound by CPI Group (UK) Ltd, Croydon, CR0 4YY

Simon & Schuster UK Ltd are committed to sourcing paper
that is made from wood grown in sustainable forests and supports the Forest
Stewardship Council, the leading international forest certification organisation.
Our books displaying the FSC logo are printed on FSC certified paper.

Mom,

Thank you for bearing the pain of childbirth.

And thank you for that one time you gave me money to join a gym for the summer, knowing full well I am incapable of growing a single ab.

Thank you for always protecting me from all the horrible things in the world.

Thank you for being my best friend,

and my rock.

This is for you . . .

Contents

Preface ◆ 1

Everything I Know About Kissing I Learned
from Winnie Cooper ◆ 3

My A-to-Z Guide to Getting Nookie in New
Delhi During High School ◆ 14

Made in England ◆ 19

King of Shuttlecocks ◆ 21

Holiday Traditions Part 1: Rakhi ◆ 33

A Thought Recorded on an Aeroplane Cocktail Napkin ◆ 35

Why Being Indian Is Cool ◆ 36

Dinners with Dad ◆ 38

Dziko and Me ◆ 52

The Art of the Head Bobble ◆ 66

Garbage, Man ◆ 68

Holiday Traditions Part 2: Dussehra ◆ 74

The Forbidden Kiss ◆ 76

Chaos Theory ◆ 83

Judgment Day in Boise ◆ 85

A Thought Recorded on an Aeroplane Cocktail Napkin ◆ 97

The Girl I Went to Mass For ◆ 98

Kumar Ran a Car ◆ 103

Lollipops and Crisps ◆ 111

The Prince and the Pauper ◆ 127

How I Knew ◆ 136

Kunal's Twelve Quick Thoughts on Dating ◆ 146

Holiday Traditions Part 3: Holi ◆ 150

Nina, Why? ◆ 152

A Thought Recorded on an Aeroplane Cocktail Napkin ◆ 165

Love's Labour's Lost ◆ 166

The Waiting Period (Extended Mix) ◆ 176

James Bond and the Mouse ◆ 189

Always Joy ◆ 196

Thirteen Things I've Learned from Playing
an Astrophysicist on TV ◆ 199

A Thought Recorded on an Aeroplane Cocktail Napkin ◆ 207

And Then I Fell in Love ◆ 208

Puppies ◆ 218

My Big Fat Indian Wedding ◆ 219

Holiday Traditions Part 4: Diwali ◆ 238

Good-bye ◆ 241

A Thought Recorded on an Aeroplane Cocktail Napkin ◆ 242

Acknowledgments ◆ 243

Yes, My
Accent
Is Real

Preface

SOMETIMES PEOPLE ASK ME, "WHY ARE YOU WRITING A MEM-oir? You're only thirty-four."

This is not a memoir. I'm not a president, or an astronaut, or a Kardashian.

This is a collection of stories from my life.

It is not an "I was born in . . ." type of book.

I was born in London and raised in New Delhi. When I was eighteen, after maneuvering my way through a billion people and a few cows,* I moved to Portland, Oregon, where I studied business, cleaned toilets, lied my way into an IT job, and fell in love twenty-seven times. I went on to get my master's in acting in Philadelphia, auditioned for a play in the basement of an Apple Store in New York City, and spent four hours a day commuting on a bus in Los Angeles. Somehow this crazy journey landed me on a little television show called *The Big Bang Theory*.

Here are some things that happened to me along the way.

---

* Obligatory cow joke. The first of many.

Everything I Know About Kissing
I Learned from Winnie Cooper

NEW DELHI, 1993. I WAS TWELVE YEARS OLD AND I HAD TWO great loves in my life. The first was Winnie Cooper from *The Wonder Years*. Cable had just come to India and I was obsessed with *Small Wonder, M*A*S*H, Doogie Howser, M.D.,* and my beloved Winnie.

My second great love was a friend of my cousin's named Ishani. She was two years older than me, she wore shorter-than-normal skirts, she smoked, and she always smelled like cigarettes and perfume. I still clearly remember that perfume—lemony but also just a little masculine, as if she'd finished her morning perfuming ritual with a splash of her father's aftershave. She had a mole like Cindy Crawford's and she was light-skinned, with hazel-brown eyes. Every guy I knew had a thing for Ishani.

But I had one advantage over the other guys: she was my cousin's best friend, and my cousin happened to live directly above me and my parents.* Whenever Ishani and my cousin would hang

---

* Many houses in New Delhi worked that way: my mom, dad, brother, and I lived on the ground floor, and my aunt, uncle, and cousin lived in a separate residence on the first floor.

out, I would follow them around like a puppy. Even though they went to the girls' school and I went to the boys', I always timed my walk from the bus so we'd somehow wind up together. *Oh, hey there, what a surprise seeing you two on this fine walk from the school bus this morning!* In the evenings I'd be there as they talked about boys and kissing and sex and stuff. Sometimes I'm not even sure if they remembered I was in the room; they would gossip and giggle while I bounced a ball off the wall. Literally. I became Ishani's good friend. A younger brother, if you will. Safe, innocent, G-rated.

"Have you ever kissed a girl?" she asked me one day.

"Never." I couldn't make eye contact. We were in my bedroom, sitting on the edge of the bed, side by side. The curtains were drawn closed, like always, to shield the room from the scorching New Delhi heat.

"*Never?*" she said, teasing.

My father was at work, my mother was taking a nap, and my cousin had gone upstairs to take a shower or something. We were alone.

Suddenly the electricity went out and the room darkened. This may sound overly convenient—and, frankly, a little implausible—but it was actually pretty common to lose power during the summers, especially in the afternoon. The government arranged something called "load shedding" to ration electricity during high-consumption months.

I could barely see her face but I could sense her next to me on the bed.

"Kiss me," she said.

I froze. My twelve-year-old self was terrified. I didn't know what to do or how to respond. *Is she joking? She must be joking. She has to be joking.*

She was not joking.

I had been dreaming of this moment for months, though I never in a million years thought it would come to pass. So of course I said the only thing that made sense: "No, no, I don't think it's the right thing."

Kunal, what are these words coming out of your mouth?

The lights came back on. She looked me in the eye and I looked away. I thought the moment had passed . . . and then, just like that, she scooted over to me and planted her lips on mine.

At that point in life, my entire knowledge of kissing came from my true love, Winnie Cooper. I had just watched the episode where Kevin and Winnie share their first kiss, sitting on a swing, and I learned one very important lesson: As Kevin leans in to kiss Winnie, he closes his eyes. And he keeps them closed the entire time. Genius.

So that's what you do when you kiss—just keep your eyes closed. Got it. Easy peasy. So when Ishani kissed me I closed my eyes, kept them shut, and I literally replayed that scene from *The Wonder Years* on an endless loop. I can't remember what I was doing with my hands, or what my mouth was doing, or even what Ishani looked or felt like in that moment. When I closed my eyes, I was Kevin Arnold, and she was Winnie Cooper.

Afterward I opened my eyes. Winnie was gone. Ishani was there.

"Okay," she said, with no inflection.

Okay.

Dry. Like it was a verdict.

Okay.

We didn't discuss the kiss. Not in that moment, not later that day, not the next day, not ever. *Okay.*

But it did happen. Clearly what we had shared was by definition special, magical, and I didn't want to rock the boat by pushing my luck for an encore.

I gave that kiss a lot of thought. Maybe too much thought. I suppose you're supposed to say that a first kiss is "lovely" or maybe "achingly sweet," but instead I thought . . . *How weird.*

I was hitting puberty and I could have been aroused by a dead duck, but even back then, on that particular day, I felt nothing. Maybe I was overthinking things. Maybe I was worried about getting the kiss right, as opposed to just living in the moment. I struggle with that a lot, you should know. Living in the moment. I should have been thinking, *Holy shit, I just kissed a girl,* and instead I'm wondering about the meaning of that noninflected, dry "*Okay.*"

So I took it upon myself and decided the most reasonable interpretation of her statement was, "*Okay,* now we're boyfriend and girlfriend."

I just assumed we were dating. We had *kissed,* right? When you're twelve, a kiss has the weight of a marriage covenant. It was my signed, sealed, delivered moment. My cousin, Ishani, and I would hang out as always after school, but now I would tell my mother, "I'm going to see my girlfriend!" Since my girlfriend liked cigarettes I decided to take up smoking, stealing little white cancer sticks from my parents so I could practice puffing.*

"We're going to a party!" my cousin said to me one day.

"What party?"

"Ishani's boyfriend's party."

I was confused. Wait, but *I'm* Ishani's boyfriend. Nervous, baffled, and hurt, I tagged along as my cousin's "plus one" to my

---

* I vomited the first time I smoked. It didn't stop me.

girlfriend's boyfriend's party. The room was filled with cool, older, dangerous-looking kids—*grown men,* really, sixteen years old— and they were drinking beer. Real beer. I scanned the crowd of giants and I spotted Ishani. With a guy. An older guy. She was holding hands with him. He was tall, with gleaming white teeth, and he wore Doc Martens, shoes that clearly meant one thing: *I'm a badass and you suck at life.* He spoke in a deep, manly voice that seemed to charm the pants off Ishani (literally, I imagined). My heart plummeted and I stared, speechless.

"Hey!" one of the bigger guys said to me. He must have caught me staring. "I'm going to kill you!"

I panicked and did the most manly thing I could think of: I ran for my life. I ran outside and he followed me. I ran faster. He still followed. Then I ran around a car to hide from him, and then, wait, wait, where'd he go—he ran right past me.

He was chasing someone else.

Who was he chasing, and why? I'll never know. But it taught me at the tender age of twelve that everything in life isn't always about you, even when you're sure it is.

I left the party alone, finally realizing that Ishani was not currently my girlfriend, had never been my girlfriend, and would never be my girlfriend. I wondered why she had kissed me in the first place. Did she see me as so innocent, so G-rated, that I didn't really count as cheating on her actual boyfriend? Or maybe *she* had never kissed anybody, and she knew she would be hanging out with these dangerous old guys, and she wanted to try it out? Maybe I was just some experiment, like a lab monkey. Or maybe she just fancied me. Or maybe she somehow sensed that while the two of us were kissing, I secretly was fantasizing about Winnie Cooper.

Okay. What a stupid word.

❖

Fast-forward seventeen years. Season three of *The Big Bang Theory*. We were prepping an episode called "The Psychic Vortex," and I picked up the script and glanced at the casting list. One name caught my eye: Danica McKellar.

The actress who played Winnie Cooper.

Holy shit. Danica was slated to play a character named Abby, and I flipped through the pages of the script to see if I would get to share any scenes with her. I learned that my character, Raj, would meet her at a party, bring her back to Sheldon's place, and then, in the episode's final scene, they would make out.

I was going to get to kiss Winnie Cooper.

And this meant only one thing: God is real.

I'd like to say that as a professional actor I was far too mature to geek out over this, but the reality is that I immediately googled her. I learned that in addition to acting, she had written well-received books about math, including *Math Doesn't Suck* and *Girls Get Curves: Geometry Takes Shape*. I also learned that she had a husband, which immediately took any actual romance off the table; that's a line I would never cross. But still, even if it's totally innocent and just pretend . . . I was going to get to kiss Winnie Cooper.

On the morning before we were to meet at the table read, I spent no more than seven hours thinking about what to wear. I decided to dress down. So, in true LA fashion, I wore a pair of expensive torn jeans, white T-shirt, sneakers, and to really complete the look, I wore one of those ridiculous LA beanies that hipsters wear in the summer. I didn't shave, because I wanted a little bit of scruff; it takes a lot of effort to show you're not expending any effort. Such is life.

I casually strolled into the table read, avoiding her, hanging around the breakfast buffet, and making small talk with the writers. I was saying things like, "Hey, Dave, really hot today, huh?"

"Um, then why are you wearing a beanie?" Dave said.

"Because I'm having a bad hair day, obviously."

Meanwhile I'm looking over his shoulder for any sight of Danica. Everybody has been to a party with "That Guy" who talks to you but really isn't interested in what you're saying; he's just saying words in your direction while scanning the crowd for more desirable company. Today, I was totally That Guy. The writers were probably thinking, *What the frack is wrong with Kunal?*

Did I want coffee? No, no coffee. I didn't want to be jittery. I wanted to be cool. Just a cool guy in a cool beanie on a hot day.

Finally I saw her . . . and she looked exactly the same as Winnie. She was perfect. She wore a white dress and had her hair up in a band. Her hair smelled like Head & Shoulders in the best possible way, though I'm sure it wasn't Head & Shoulders.

I introduced myself. "Hi, I play Raj, my name is Kunal." Funny that I said that in reverse. "That's me," I said, pointing to my assigned seat at the table, which had a big card that read "Kunal" on it. I tried not to giggle like a schoolgirl.

She smiled, we made some chitchat, and for the most part I avoided saying anything creepy. We sat next to each other at the table. When the director introduced the guest actors for that week's episode, I clapped harder than everyone else when her name was announced, and nudged her with my elbow. *Dork.* During a table read you don't actually kiss, but when we did get to that blessed scene in the script, I did a silent happy dance for myself. You know that dance, the one you do in your heart, just for yourself, for no one else to see.

I spent most of the week hogging her time, chatting, soaking up every second of her glorious smile. "I understand that you've written a bunch of math books," I said casually, not mentioning that I found this out through Google at 2 a.m. "It's so nice that you're on the show, because we have a big following of math and science fans." Was I laying it on a little thick? Maybe. But anything was better than getting nervous and blurting out, "Danica, oh sweet Danica, the first time I ever kissed a girl I closed my eyes and pretended I was kissing you, and I fantasized about you for most of my boyhood and sometimes still do even now in my adult life."

And honestly, even though I had this massive crush, it's still my TV show (along with the rest of the cast and crew, of course), and when someone is my guest, I'm going to take care of that person. I want them to be at ease. I want them to be comfortable. I was just happy to be a butterfly in her lovely presence.

❖

Kiss Day was Thursday, during the show's run-through. They served Lebanese for lunch—hummus, tabouli, tzatziki—yummy!—*Hell no, I'm not touching any of that!* I even avoided coffee so I wouldn't have coffee breath, and then I popped seventeen Altoids. My brain hatched all these scenarios of things going tragically wrong: she'd be repulsed by my breath, I'd be overly aggressive, or maybe accidentally miss the target and kiss her on her nose or left ear or eyelid. . . .

And then the moment arrived. No more excuses. It was time for the big scene. Sheldon enters the apartment, he doesn't get along with his date, and then Abby sits on Raj's lap. (*She's sitting on my lap!*) As soon as the director says "Action!" we're supposed to start kissing. While Sheldon is talking to his date, Danica and I *have* to kiss for the entire time in the background. (Note to the writer of this episode: I owe you a Rolex.)

"Aaaaaaaaaand . . . action!" said the director.

Before he even finished saying "And," we started kissing.

Allow me to point out that stage kissing, in itself, comes with an inviolable and highly sophisticated set of rules that must be honored 100 percent of the time. The number-one rule of stage kissing: No Tongue Without Permission.* There was no way I was going to push the boundaries or do anything disrespectful, so I erred on the side of caution and kept my lips sealed like a fish. It was a long, loooooong kiss.

Take two! We kissed again. Take three! We kissed again. And again. And again. When it was all said and done, we did six takes. And, to be honest, I was kissed out.

Okay!

I don't have any illusions that it meant anything more than just a stage kiss, as she was married and she's a pro. This is what pros do. They make out passionately and pretend to fall in love with each other and then they go home to their happy wives and husbands. That said, I do happen to know that exactly nine months later, Danica had a baby. Did she race straight home from our kiss and make passionate, unrestrained love to her husband? I'm not saying that's what happened; I'm just saying we have no evidence that that *didn't* happen.

"You know, this might sound funny," I finally told her the next day, "but I have you to thank for my very first kiss."

---

* Though on occasion you can probably get away with 10 percent tongue.

She looked at me. Those eyes. "Really? How?"

I told her a short version of the story, playing up the angle of "I learned to close my eyes from your scene with Kevin," and glossing over the specific facts of "I visualized you and replayed the scene on an endless loop."

"That's a really cute story," she said, much to my relief.

Look, all these years later, I'm still in love with Winnie Cooper. I think *every* guy born between 1974 and 1985 is still in love with her. But it got me thinking. More than just Winnie, and Danica, and the stage kiss we shared, more than the beanie and the coffee and the seventeen Altoids, I just can't stop thinking about how life comes full circle. There are forces in this universe that are beyond our control; they're nonlinear, and they can't be explained by science or mathematics. You see, just as I thought about Winnie Cooper when I kissed Ishani, I thought about Ishani when I kissed Winnie Cooper. It brought back that memory of us sitting side by side on the bed, of the lights flickering on and off, of that twelve-year-old boy who knew so little of the world.

I hadn't thought of Ishani—my first crush, the first girl who broke my heart—in years. So after the Winnie Kiss I wondered what had become of her. I searched for her on Facebook, I googled, I asked my cousin about her. It turns out that she married one of the seniors from my high school, a kid who wore Doc Martens and smoked cigarettes out the window of our school bus. I wonder if she's happy. I wonder if she'll read this. I wonder if she ever thinks about our kiss.

And as for Danica? She was recently on *Dancing with the Stars*, and to the surprise of no one, she still looks incredible. She was partnered with the dancing coach Valentin Chmerkovskiy. I can't help but wonder if perhaps, twenty years ago, Valentin Chmerkovskiy saw an episode of *The Wonder Years* in which Kevin danced with Winnie for the first time, and if when twelve-year-old Valentin danced with a girl for the very first time, he closed his eyes and thought of Winnie Cooper. Maybe life came full circle for him, too.

My A-to-Z Guide to Getting Nookie in New Delhi During High School

MY CHILDHOOD WAS SPENT IN AN ALL-BOYS SCHOOL. NOTH-ing about that is cool. We basically stood around and scratched our balls and thought about girls and giggled. Girls were never around. And what happens when girls aren't around? Boys begin to act like maniacal hooligans. We were so full of pent-up sexual aggression that we took it out on each other by playing a game called "India and Pakistan," which, I suppose, is sort of like "Cowboys and Indians," except instead of make-believe whooping and yelling, we threw actual stones at each other. My face was hit by many rocks. (Which is probably why today I play an astrophysicist and not Romeo.)

Just as in America we also had science fair projects, but in our school we had to actually *present* our work in front of the entire student body, giving a speech about hydropowered generators or whatever. In theory, the rest of the students would listen to the presentation, admire the hard work, and ask insightful follow-up questions to further our understanding. In reality, we used this as an opportunity to ask questions to screw up the presenter. We took notes, looked for weaknesses, and tried to figure out the trickiest question that would stump them. One year this kid gave a presentation on, well, hydropowered generators. I scribbled notes and worked on a good *Gotcha!* question. After forty-five minutes I raised my hand and asked, "So, what exactly *is* a 'hydropowered generator'?"

The kid didn't blink. Calmly he said, "If you had listened to the presentation, then you would know what it was, so obviously you weren't paying attention."

The crowd let out a collective "ooooooooooooh." I had just gotten a smackdown. At least there weren't any girls around. Because we didn't have any interaction with women, our only hope was to organize PG-rated parties at each other's houses, invite the one girl we knew (she had a mustache and helped out with cricket practice), and then ask her to bring her friends from the adjoining all-girls school. This often resulted in a ratio of forty-five guys to two girls. And one of them was almost a dude. All we did was dance in one big awkward circle. Everyone was too scared to talk to the girls, really, so we tried to win their affections with superhuman feats of endurance and strength.

"Who can drink this Coca-Cola the fastest?"

"I can!"

"No, I can!"

"I can!"

"One, two, three, go!"

We jumped onto a table and guzzled a bottle of Coke, somehow convinced that if we drank it the fastest, the girls would melt with desire. *Watch me. Want me.* Chug, chug, chug . . . I chugged that damn Coke so fast that it exploded through my nose, sending saliva, snot, and blood everywhere. Ever had a nosebleed from Coca-Cola? I did. I think it was even coming out of my eyes.

The two girls were grossed out and I never saw them again. Who cares? They were probably weirdos anyway.

"How many cartwheels can you do?!" someone asked at another party.

"Let's see who can jump the highest!"

"Who can do the most push-ups?!"

It was sort of like medieval times, or what I know of medieval times from Disney cartoons, where you hope to woo the village maiden through manly acts of valor. It never worked, though, because I can't imagine any girl ever thinking, *I wonder which boy can jump the highest? I wanna get with HIM tonight.*

The camaraderie in an all-boys school is epic. We really felt a sense of brotherhood. So when the seniors graduated each year, it was a very emotional moment. The juniors would throw the seniors a good-bye party. In my junior year, about four girls came to this party, which made us very proud, and I gave a speech to honor the graduates.

"We'll always love you, we'll miss you, and we have a special song for you," I said, wiping back tears. Then I motioned for the DJ to play Diddy's "I'll Be Missing You." Diddy had just played that song at the MTV Movie Awards, and in the video he does this dance where he looks like a penguin who opens his wings to flap out the excess water. We all did that slow Penguin Dance together in unison, and then some of the junior boys took the senior boys on their shoulders, swaying back and forth in an emotional ballad. *I'll be missing you. . . .* I looked around and saw all four of the girls shaking their heads at us, thinking, *What the shit did I get myself into?* It was basically this massive room of guys crying, dancing like penguins, and bro-ing out to P. Diddy. End. Of. Scene.

On the off chance that we met girls, I had an A-to-Z Guide to Getting Nookie in New Delhi:

A. I see a pretty girl (or any girl) dancing in a group at a party.

B. I begin to dance closer to her group of friends, inching my way to the center.

C. I reach the center of the group and take steps dancing toward said girl, and then back away while still dancing. If she is interested, she dances toward me as I back away. We go back and forth like this.

D. After song I introduce myself and meet her friends.

E. My other friends approach and we all set a movie date for both groups of friends to go out together.

F. During group movie date, said girl and I magically find ourselves sitting together.

G. Elbows touch.

H. Reach for popcorn at same time girl does.

I. Hold hands inside popcorn.

J. During the movie, maneuver thigh until it touches girl's resting hand.

K. Close eyes and dream.

L. After thigh touch we are now dating.

M. Endless phone chatting ensues.

N. More group movie dates.

O. Bunk school (play hooky) and end up at friend's empty house.

P. Go into a guest bedroom and lock door.

Q. Fill bathtub with soap and hot water.

R. Take bath together with all clothes on.

S. Kiss on cheek.

T. Move to neck.

U. Move to lips.

V. Rub hands on body (over clothes).

W. Friend's parents come home, bath time ends.

X. Parents find out about bunking, no more baths.

Y. More group movie dates.

Z. Break up. . . . It has been three years. Return immediately to Step A.

Made in England

HAVE I MENTIONED THAT I WAS ACTUALLY BORN IN ENGLAND?
I was two weeks premature and a C-section (sorry about that,
Mom).* It was April 30, 1981, a Thursday, I believe. Rainy probably,
because it was Hounslow, which is in London, close to Heathrow
Airport. The Indian ghetto, if you will.

I was just four years old when my parents decided it was time
to go back to India and take care of their parents. So, my memories
of England are quite limited. I'm not one of those eidetic memory
people like Sheldon on *The Big Bang Theory*. But I do specifically
remember waiting by the window for Dad to come home from
work. I had this blue onesie that was softer than a baby's bottom,
and I wore it all the time. It was so soft that it even doubled as a
blanket. We had this big window that overlooked the street. I remember crawling up onto the sofa and standing just tall enough
to peek over the windowsill. I'm not sure babies can tell time, but
in my memory I could feel when it was getting close. I guess my
brain was the size of dog's brain, and they can tell when it's time

---

* I would use the term *Caesarean*, but it makes me think too much of a certain
salad.

for their master to come home, so surely there is some correlation. When I spotted Dad from a distance I would begin to make all sorts of sounds and noises, probably saying things like "Dad's comingggg hommmeeeee yeeeeaaaaahhhhhhh," but what really came out was "googoo gaga."

And that is all.

That was England.

King of Shuttlecocks

WHEN I TELL PEOPLE THAT I PLAYED BADMINTON GROWING up they laugh at me and call me girly. Because, I guess, in America badminton is a sport played by girls in their grandmother's backyard. I mean there is some merit in laughing at a sport in which the object you hit is called a "birdie," or more correctly, a "shuttlecock." Yes, the ball of badminton is called a shuttlecock. Shuttle-cock. But I still played it with fervor. And you may not believe me, but I even picked up chicks while showing off my badminton moves. I swear.

My family had joined a private club, aptly called "Friends Club," because it was located in an area called "Friends Colony," which wasn't really a colony of friends; it was just, I don't know, a neighborhood. Anyway. This Friends Club had tennis courts, squash courts, a gym, a musty old English-type pub, a pool, and an indoor badminton court. At first I played tennis but the courts were too damn crowded, so I switched to badminton since it capitalized on my ninjalike agility and superior hand-eye coordination.* They kept the courts indoors, with basically no air-conditioning or

---

* Translation: it's the only sport where it didn't matter that I was weak.

ventilation. And have I mentioned that New Delhi is hot as balls? So what you think of as this "grandmother sport" was played in a 120-degree sauna with 95 percent humidity. You basically played the game in a sticky pool of sweat.

Quickly I became good—they called me the Tiger Woods of badminton. Which is a lie. I had a flamboyant playing style where I dove for birdies that were easily within reach, and sometimes, just for kicks, I intentionally lost points so I could stage a dramatic comeback. Women love underdogs, after all, and the girls would come from the pool to watch our heroics. This gave me a jolt of self-confidence and boosted my social standing. I knew I was good when "Gap and Guess Girl," a girl who earned her nickname by, well, always wearing shorts from the Gap and Guess, graced us with her lovely presence. (She later ended up stalking me; long story.)

I should mention that this club also served food. And among the many delectable items was one very special dish called "cheese-balls." Let's examine this for a second. Cheese-balls. Balls of cheese. Fried. Served with spicy powder and ketchup. And Indian ketchup is already spicy. So fried balls of cheese, spicy masala, and spicy ketchup, all washed down with an ice-cold lemonade. One month I ate cheeseballs every day. Cheeseballs in my face, after shuttlecocks and chicks. I think when I die I want that on my tombstone. "RIP Kunal Nayyar: Shuttlecock-smashing Romeo, died for love of cheeseballs."

Another cheeseball was a guy who worked at the courts, a man we called "the Marker," who was the laziest drunk I've ever seen. A slender guy with a big potbelly, he'd been an excellent badminton player years before, or so he said, but now he just coasted on his reputation and spent most of his afternoons sleeping on benches.

"Kunal, my house burnt down," he told me once.

"Oh my God, that's terrible."

"Do you think your family could help me out?" he asked.

"But wait . . . Didn't your house burn down last summer?"

He told me forty-three times that his house burnt down. He also drank whiskey like it was Gatorade. During the afternoons he was supermean and grumpy to the kids, but at 7 p.m., when the adults entered the club, he suddenly perked up and became joyful and happy. (The adults, unlike us, had money and would tip.)

But the Marker was a saint, I suppose, compared to this sixteen-year-old kid who was rumored to be doing drugs and sleeping with prostitutes. He was the court's bully, sometimes smacking the younger kids in the face with his racket. Supposedly he was part of some gang. He was a handsome chap and had nice hair, except his thumb had an extra finger growing out of it. We called him Six Fingers.

One day Six Fingers was picking on the younger kids, like always, but this time one of them, my friend Addy, talked back to him. Addy was in the middle of a match and Six Fingers basically stormed the court and told the youngsters to get lost so he could play. Addy had had enough of the bullying and decided not to leave.

Six Fingers slapped him in the face. Hard. He drew blood and Addy had to go home.

The next day, and I have no idea where this courage came from, I confronted Six Fingers.

"Yesterday, when you slapped Addy, that wasn't right."

Six Fingers gave me a hard look. His eyes were tinged with red. People didn't talk to Six Fingers like this. He inched closer to me. I stood my ground. He moved a little closer and I could smell his rotten breath.

Then he said something to me in Hindi that crudely translates to "Do you have an insect inside you?"

Huh? I told him I did not.

"Should I take it out?"

"No, I don't have an insect inside me, so no reason for you to take it out."

This was his way of telling me not to cross the line with him. My badminton skills, and the fact that some of the older guys liked having me on their team, were the only thing that prevented me from getting a racket shoved up my ass. This, however, was my last and only warning. Insect? I still don't really get it.

The episode strengthened my friendship with Addy, who quickly became my top rival, the Nadal to my Federer. And the dude could really play. He's five five, a little shorter than me, but stocky and strong. Addy also happened to have an exceptionally square head, which made him look like a real-life bobblehead doll.

Addy was a smasher. This was his great advantage. He was less nimble but he played with so much power—he could smash the shuttlecock to my feet. He played with force; I played with finesse. A classic case of the Irresistible Force versus the Immovable Object . . . I watch too many movies.

One day the club hired a new swimming coach. He was Israeli, eighteen years old, this good-looking guy who wore tiny swim trunks and had the first six-pack I'd ever seen. He had no body hair. Every girl had a crush on him and maybe I did, too. We became friends and he showed me some moves from Krav Maga, the Israeli martial arts, and I learned a few punches and kicks. I told him about Hindi culture and he taught me about Israeli food. I idolized him. It was almost like a summer bromance.

Leon was vague and mysterious about his past, and I sensed that he had been through some shit. One evening he called our home to say that he would not be coming back to Friends Club, ever.

"Some problems with . . . the authorities," he said cryptically.

"Are you okay?" I could feel the panic in my voice.

"I'm a little beat up," he said, and then I learned that he was officially accused of stealing, though the charges were bullshit. It turns out that he had fallen in love with a seventeen-year-old girl, and when the girl's father and brothers found out, they accused him of stealing and then broke his arm and gave him two black eyes. After he told me all this on the phone I turned to my parents, asking if they could take me to the club.

"We're in the middle of dinner, Kunal."

"But he's been beaten up. I have to see him."

"We're eating!"

"He has two black eyes! I need to see him!" I began crying, and my parents were baffled. Why did I care so much that this guy had been beaten up?

"You can see him tomorrow," my mother said.

They didn't understand the depths of my feelings, and I'm not sure I did, either. My brother eventually drove me to the Friends Club after dinner, and I saw Leon and his black eyes. We took a quiet stroll around the club, reminiscing about how fun the summer had been. He told me he was being deported back to Israel. I think I kind of loved him. The pool never did seem quite the same after he left. I wonder where he is today. It's funny how, as kids and teenagers, we have friendships and relationships that, at the time, feel like the most cherished bonds of our lives, and then, as the years go by, we find ways to replace the irreplaceable. And maybe, when my parents were confused by my tears, they actually *weren't* that confused. Maybe they understood perfectly. Maybe they knew that, yes, I would be stung by the end of this friendship, but that this is part of life, and I would go through these kinds of breakups, like all of us, again and again and again.

❖

In 1996 we had the first inaugural Friends Club Badminton Tournament. I was fifteen and at the peak of my prowess on the court. The whole club community and neighborhood turned out for this grand championship. My parents were there. And all my cousins. And my grandparents, brother, and friends. Even Six Fingers was in the crowd and cheering us on. For a second I even wondered if Leon might be somewhere in the crowd. I cruised through my first few opponents—Federer in the openings rounds of Wimbledon— and faced my first real challenge in the semifinals, where I played a dude who looked like Scorpion from Mortal Kombat, like he always had a mask over his face even though he never wore a mask. You could only see his eyes and these eyes told you *nothing.* He tested me at first but I won the match in straight sets, sending me to the greatest showdown of my young career: the Badminton Championship Match.

My opponent? Addy, of course. Everyone had expected to see Addy and me in the finals; this is what the crowd had paid to watch. (Well, no one actually paid anything.) Nadal versus Federer. Foreman versus Ali. Skywalker versus Vader. It was the biggest match of my life, and, I suppose, this was my first real moment on a stage. The crowd whispered in anticipation, nervous, and I imagined them on the edge of their seats, almost afraid of the match they were about to witness, a duel between two friends that would make one a legend, the other a shell of his former self.*

We knew each other's games very well. I won the coin toss and chose to serve first. Badminton is the best of three games, and each game goes to fifteen points. Everyone in that stadium (yes, in my mind, we were in a stadium) knew that I had one killer weapon: my drop shot. Instead of sending the birdie deep I could flick it just slightly over the net, making it damn near impossible to return. With Addy, though, I had to change my strategy. A drop shot is a double-edged sword: yes, it might win you a point if your opponent is too far away to get to it, but if they *do* reach the birdie in time, you've just made the mistake of inviting them to the net, and once they're at the net, they're in prime position to smash the next point. And Addy, of course, was the ultimate smasher. The drop shot was too risky—I had to put it on ice.

I served first. I had a flamboyant style of serving, dropping the shuttlecock from high above my head with an absurdly long windup. When I served I tried to push him back as far as I could, which, theoretically, would neutralize his smashing advantage.

The first point was a thirty-seven-shot rally, and it set the tone for the entire match. Neither of us gave an inch. Since I pushed him back he did the same to me, which led to exceptionally long rallies. We both played toward the back of the court. Addy was better at targeting my backhand, which is weaker, so my shots came dan-

---

* I now realize that our parents were actually saying to each other, "Oh, what nice exercise these boys are getting! Such a healthy pastime."

gerously close to sailing out of bounds. My plan backfired. I was pushing too hard, aiming too close to the back of the court, and it cost me several points.

I lost the first game 15–11.

We had a quick break and I sipped a family concoction of lemonade spiked with electrolyte powder, given to me by my mother in a beautiful steel flask. I felt exhausted and low and beaten. While I guzzled the juice, someone tapped my shoulder.

The drunkard Marker, who managed the courts.

He whispered his whiskey breath into my ear, "Why aren't you using your drop shot?"

"I can't. He'll smash it," I said.

"That's your game. Play your game. Play your strength," the Marker said, then quietly slipped away. (*Wait, he knew my game? Maybe all his napping was just a ruse, and he was secretly a badminton Yoda.*)

I had new fire in my eyes. I decided, *Fuck it, he's right. I'm going to play my game.*

On the first point of the second game I unleashed my drop shot . . . and it caught him off guard. One to zero, Kunal. I could suddenly smell the fear. He had been lulled into staying too far to the back, and once I had the drop shot working he was slow to recover. Drop shot after drop shot, each one a perfect little arc that dribbled over the net. I won the second game 15–9. (I saw Gap and Guess Girl in the crowd and gave her a wink.)

Game three. Easily the biggest moment in the history of Friends Club, and perhaps the biggest moment in the history of Indian sport competition.

At this point we are too exhausted to really be thinking strategy. It is just flat-out war. The crowd gasps after each and every point, and I am too tired to do my usual showman's trick of diving for birdies that are easily within reach. Just point after point after point, back and forth, drop shots and smashes, deep shots, long rallies, short rallies, and we're both dripping with sweat. You have to understand that badminton is a sport that's *fast*. You're running all the time. Yes, the court is smaller than a tennis court, but the difference is that as soon as you hit the shuttlecock *it comes right back to you,* meaning that you're sprinting left, right, backward, forward, every three seconds. Go watch some badminton on YouTube—you'll see.

Finally, at the end of this marathon game, the score is tied 14–14 (because of course it is).

When the game is tied, to win the match you have to win by a difference of two points. I win the next point, so it's 15–14.

Match point.

If I win this I become the champion. So, I fake a serve that looks like it will go toward the back of the court . . . and then I drop it in front. Drop shot.

Addy sees it. He gets to it. *He got there.* Then he hits this beautiful drop shot of his own, right in front of the net, and flicks his wrist to put a spin on the shuttlecock so that it wobbles as it falls, making it nearly impossible to return.

My only option at this point is to desperately scoop the birdie into the air, with no control or power, which would lob back to him in the easiest shot he had seen all day. My. Only. Option. So I do it. I watch as the shuttlecock rises slowly, slowly, sloooooooowwwww-wwly setting him up for the perfect smash. I have just given him a Christmas gift.

He has all the time in the world. He pulls the racket back for a smash, whooshes it forward . . . and smashes the birdie into the net.

Sixteen to fourteen, Kunal.

I have won.

I am the Badminton Champion of the World.

❖

The next day I got out of bed and it felt like there wasn't any fluid in my body. Every muscle was in so much pain. I was a little embarrassed at the way I celebrated the victory—double-fist pumping as if I had just won Wimbledon—but glad that at least I shook Addy's hand and congratulated him on a hard-fought game. Oddly, though, the victory didn't come with elation. It brought me a dose of guilt. I won that final point on Addy's unforced error, and it felt like a lousy way to triumph. I flipped on the TV to catch the U.S. Open Final between Pete Sampras and Andre Agassi, and I couldn't even watch *them* play, as the sight of them running made my own legs tired. I called Addy to see how he was doing.

"Kunal, you won't believe this, but I'm watching the U.S. Open and I'm too tired to even watch Agassi run."

We both laughed about the coincidence, took naps, and then somehow mustered enough energy for the afternoon's trophy ceremony. Gracious as always, Addy suggested that I say a few words.

A few words? Sure, you bet, I'll say a few words. I wrote an entire speech that began, "In the year 1996 badminton was recorded as the fastest sport in the world. . . ." It was one of *those*. I literally spoke for twenty-six minutes—no joke. This is thirteen minutes longer than Martin Luther King's "I Have a Dream" speech. It's twenty-four minutes longer than the Gettysburg Address. I thanked Addy and my parents and the Marker and all my competitors and the girls in their swimsuits and the entire 17 billion people of India; there's even a good chance I thanked you, dear reader.

For some reason a year later, in the second annual tournament, they did not invite the winner to give a speech. Or, more technically, they did not allow *me* to give a speech, as I won the thing again. The tournament changed over time. You would think the tournament would get bigger and bigger, but for some reason, it was never quite the same. In future years they spent more money and bought a fancier trophy and installed an electronic leaderboard, but we never could recapture that original pixie dust.

Or maybe the tournament stayed the same and *I* had changed. After I had won the championship, I entered an *actual tournament* that was held in an actual stadium used for the Olympic qualifiers. This wasn't a "social club," this was legit. Real players who trained with real coaches. In the first round I was matched up against the number-one player in New Delhi, a kid named Pinky, and I looked at this kid and realized he was poor. Dad had taken me to the game. I remember looking at Pinky's shoes, which were falling apart; he wore a dirty T-shirt; and he didn't have a fancy steel flask with lemonade and electrolytes. Pinky destroyed me in that first game 15–2. In the break before the second set I looked at Pinky in his dirty shoes, and Dad offered me the steel casket and I didn't drink from it—I was so embarrassed by my beautiful thermos that I didn't drink any fluids at all. In the second game I played as hard as I could, determined to win this scrappy kid's respect . . . and lost the second game 15–9.

"Who's your coach?" Pinky asked afterward.

I told him I didn't have one.

"Wait, then where do you take lessons?"

"I've never taken a lesson."

Pinky looked at me a little differently, shook my hand, and that was enough. I had played with the best and lost. Maybe that was enough for me and badminton, period. My enthusiasm eventually waned. I still dove for the shuttlecocks to impress the Gap and Guess Girl, but by the time of the third annual tournament, as a senior my heart just wasn't in it. Once again I reached the finals, this time to face Scorpion. I had a chance to win the tournament—which would give me a threepeat—but on match point, when I had an easy smash, I whiffed it into the net. (Somewhere Addy must have been laughing.) Karma's a bitch. That's okay, though—in a few months I would head to America to start college and begin a very different chapter in my life. I was almost *thankful* to lose that third finals. Looking back on it, I guess I felt sort of like LeBron in the 2014 NBA Finals, who, after being on top for so long, seemed worn down by the grind. Yup, me and LeBron—we're basically the same person.

Grandmother sport, my ass.

Curling, on the other hand . . .

Holiday Traditions Part 1: Rakhi

Rakhi (*RA-kee*): *n.* annual Indian holiday honoring the
bonds between siblings, close relatives, and friends.

RAKHI IS AN ANNUAL INDIAN TRADITION THAT IS MEANT TO
strengthen the bond between brothers and sisters. This is my favorite Indian festival because the ceremony is so beautiful: your
sister, or your female cousin, or even just a girl who you *think of* as
a sister—or who thinks of you as a brother—ties a little decorated
thread, also known as a Rakhi, around your wrist. This symbol-
izes that she is praying for your long life, and once you accept this
Rakhi, you have to protect her from all the evil in the world forever.
It is a lifelong pledge of protection.

There are, however, two problems with this lovely tradition.
The first is that I have nineteen cousins in nineteen different
homes. So when I was a kid this was a very stressful day, as I had
to race from house to house and keep adding new threads. When
your sister ties this ribbon on your hand it is also customary for
her to feed you chocolate as a blessing, and in return, I have to give
her an envelope with some cash. So after nineteen threads I'm not
only broke as shit, I'm also ready to vomit from being force-fed too
much chocolate. Still, though, I took pride in having so many cous-

ins and quasi-sisters who needed my manly protection, and the next day at school I flashed my wrist full of threads, flaunting it like bling. Do you know the rapper 2 Chainz? I was like 19 Rakhiz.

Then there's the second problem: what if you want to hook up with a girl, and she asks you if she can tie you a Rakhi? It's over. This is her ultimate way of saying "Oh, Kunal, I will always see you as my brother!" The Rakhi band is no joke—it's not something you can undo. I took it very seriously. So, a few days before the holiday, I would hide from all these girls and pretend that I was sick and refuse to answer their calls.

Rakhi (*RA-kee*): *n.* 1. annual Indian holiday honoring the bonds between siblings, close relatives, and friends. 2. The ultimate cock-block. See also *Rakh-block.*

A Thought Recorded on an Aeroplane* Cocktail Napkin

IT IS IMPOSSIBLE TO DRINK COLD WATER AND CHEW MINT GUM AT THE SAME TIME.

---

* Not a typo.

Why Being Indian Is Cool

DEAR READER, I KNOW WHAT YOU'RE THINKING: *KUNAL, YOU seem awesome and we should totally hang out sometime, but being Indian is soooooo not cool.*

Now, I don't mean to throw my own culture under the bus, but if anyone is allowed to say it, it's me; I mean, I *am* Indian. And dear reader, you're right. We are not a nation of cool. We are not cool like the French, or the Italians, or anyone from South America. I'm not saying we're entirely useless. We are known for some really good stuff, like medicine, engineering, and spicy food. But if you put us in a thong on a beach in Rio . . .

Everything came to India a little late. You may remember a few of my favorite TV shows growing up—*Small Wonder, M*A*S*H, Doogie Howser, M.D.,* and *The Wonder Years.* So when I moved to the States for college in 1999, all of my cultural references were about thirteen years behind the curve. I'd say things like, "Did you guys hear the new Bryan Adams song?" I worshipped true artists like UB40 and Mariah Carey. I could sing every word from "(Everything I Do) I Do It for You."* I could even air-guitar the solo with one hand while playing air piano with the other. *Recognize.*

---

* Aka the stirring love theme from *Robin Hood: Prince of Thieves.*

Or take fashion. Even when I would try to dress cool, I'd still be held back by my Indianness. I might wear a great pair of jeans and a nice polo shirt, but under that polo you'd see a white undershirt. That means a shirt under a shirt. Think about that when it's 120 degrees Fahrenheit and 99 percent humidity. When I went to the gym, my socks were pulled up to my knees and my shorts were so tight that if I bent over you would see some butt cheek, and maybe even the outline of my testes.* Despite my best efforts, my suit pants would often be a little too short, my shirts a little too shiny.

Then, a few years ago, I noticed something really strange had happened. I noticed that retailers everywhere—from American Apparel to Barneys—had started stealing *my* look for *their* stores. Turns out that we Indians were hipsters before hipsters were even invented. Indians love big mustaches and thick-rimmed glasses. We love pocket calculators and pocket squares. We smell like musk and talcum and the earth but have the latest high-tech toys in our pockets. Today the coolest thing is to appear to be totally unconcerned with what's cool. And I can't help but wonder if we indeed are suddenly actually cool.

It's as if the entire fashion world has run out of ideas, only to begin recycling itself, leaving us, us Indians, at the forefront of cool. We were the original hipsters, with our facial hair and old-fashioned sensibilities. In a sense, we are the rise of the anti-cool movement that has in some roundabout way transformed us, actually, into a nation of cool.

So to my Indian brothers and sisters, I say: Be proud and know that you are now cutting-edge. But don't get used to it. This is fashion, so it will all change again soon.

---

* Short for testicles, especially in short shorts.

Dinners with Dad

WHEN I WAS GROWING UP, IT WAS A TRUTH UNIVERSALLY AC-
knowledged that every night at eight thirty, no exceptions, we had
to be seated at the dining room table for dinner. This was the one
absolute law that my father enforced. No TV, no phone calls, no
texting or Twitter or Facebook (in those days, it was more like no
Walkman or pager or Game Boy). And no eating in silence, either.
We were *forced* to share about our day. About what we'd been
doing, how classes were, anything new that we had learned. Now,
at the time I was pretty young, around ten years old, and as such
these dinners could often seem tedious and boring. But the truth
is, some of my greatest life lessons came from sitting around that
solid mahogany dining table, a table that had once belonged to
my grandfather's grandfather. It had been around when the British
took us over, and stood strong when we got our freedom. I always
hoped that table could come to life and join these conversations.
I'll bet it would have a lot of wisdom to share. For a table.*

Conversations would start trivially, maybe about school or
about cricket. But then Dad would move on to something deeper;

---

* Of course, it's beds that really know what's what.

usually a topic that would bring up questions of morality and ethics, or why people of the same religion would turn on each other, or why we thought war existed. Heavy stuff. Or we would start by chatting about why one of my aunts was mad at my uncle, and this would segue into a discussion about personal morality. We talked a lot about relationships of all kinds, those between parents and children, or teachers and students, or friends and neighbors. My dad was always curious about humans, about how we react in different situations. He asked us hard questions at a young age, and even better, he listened carefully and respectfully when we answered. He could have dismissed our answers by claiming we were just children. But he always gave us respect; he really did make us feel like our ideas counted. And Dad wasn't just some preachy old professor of philosophy. He was mad cool. He wore slim suits and had a handlebar mustache and Ray-Ban sunglasses—he was like the Original OG. Which I guess would make him the Original Original Gangster.

Here are some things he taught me.*

IF WHAT YOU WANT HAPPENS, GOOD. IF IT DOESN'T HAPPEN, *VERY GOOD.*

When you want something really badly in life and it doesn't pan out the way you envisioned, you really only have two options:

1. You give up and you get dejected and you shit on yourself.

2. You realize that every failure is an opportunity. It's something you can learn from.

---

* Note: Should you choose to follow any or all of this advice, the author and publisher are not responsible for the consequences.

I've experienced so many setbacks in life. I suppose all of us have. But this is probably the best advice I've ever been given, because it's simple and useful and true.

If it happens, GOOD. If it doesn't happen, VERY GOOD.

THERE ARE TWO SIDES TO EVERY STORY.

Empathy at a young age is a great remedy for confusion. Even and in fact especially when it seems like the other side is absolutely wrong. (Which is in most cases, since we always think we're right. Right?) In 1993, tensions between Hindus and Muslims flared up and literally surrounded us. Riots erupted just outside our neighborhood; we could hear the police sirens and see smoke from various fires around the city. Dad had such a strong sense of morality that even at that moment, amid all the chaos, he still pushed us to be empathetic. "Even though we are Hindu, Kunal, we must recognize that the Muslims feel just as strongly about their religion and their cause. And they also deserve the basic human rights we have. Why else would they be willing to die for their beliefs?"

USE A SPREADSHEET.

Dad was an accountant, so I knew how to use Excel before I knew how to unhook a bra. Everything had to fall within a budget, and all expenses and cash outflow as well as inflow had to be perfectly balanced in the spreadsheet. And to be honest, to this day spreadsheets still drive me bat-shit crazy. But using them has saved my ass again and again. Even as a naïve college freshman, my spreadsheet told me that if I spent too much on eating and going out, I wouldn't have enough money to buy underwear. (So I didn't. Buy underwear, that is.) So do your spreadsheets, everyone, lest you be left naked underneath your pants.

DISARM WITH A SMILE.

Valentine's Day was a big deal when I was young. The year I finally had a girlfriend in Ishani (or so I thought), I naturally wanted to get her something really nice. It was going to be my first Valentine's Day gift to my first girlfriend, so of course I carefully selected the one thing every girl wants: an electronic card that plays a tinny version of "I Will Always Love You" when you open it. They sold these at Archie's Gallery, a popular gift shop named after the comic book of the same name. *Archie* comics were huge in India. I never could figure out exactly why. But anyway . . .

I found the card and handed the clerk a hundred rupees, which is the equivalent of two dollars.

"I need more," said the clerk.

"What?"

"The card is a hundred and sixty rupees."

"Oh. I don't have any more money. I won't buy it, then."

"No, you already bought it. See, it's in your hand. You need to give me sixty more rupees," the clerk said. He was being a dick and I wasn't having it.

"I'm going to call my father!" I said, raising my voice. "We live down the street. He won't stand for the way you're treating me."

"Okay, call him, we'll see what happens," the clerk said.

I called my father, sniffling and blubbering, "You won't believe it, Dad. They're not giving me my money back. They are acting like thieves."

"I'll be there soon," my dad said.

At this point, the manager and the security guard had moved to the front of the store, nervous about what force might come barging through the door. A few minutes later my dad showed up and I gave them a smug smile, knowing that Dad would rip them a new one. *You messed with the wrong twelve-year-old.*

My dad comes in without saying a word and just smiles at them. A big, warm smile. He has two of the deepest dimples I have ever seen on his cheeks, which gives his smile the power to disarm a thousand Archie's Gallery guards. It puts everyone at ease. "I'm sorry for the confusion, gentlemen. How much more do we owe you?"

"Sir, just sixty rupees."

"Okay. Here's sixty rupees," my dad said, paying them. "Any more problems? Is this all sorted?"

"Thank you, sir. Yes, we're all good here, we are sorry."

We left the store and I looked at him, betrayed. "Dad, what happened? I thought you were going to kick their asses!"

My dad looked at me.

"Kunal, how much did the card cost?"

"A hundred and sixty rupees."

"How much did you pay them?"

"One hundred."

"Okay, then between the two of us, we paid for it."

Two sides. One smile to bridge the gap.*

---

* To this day, I still wish (just a little bit) that he hadn't smiled and had kicked their asses. But that's not the point of the story.

BUY A HOUSE YOU CAN AFFORD.

If you buy something that's too expensive, then you won't have enough leftover money to go out and enjoy yourself, so what's the point? You want to sit in an empty house all alone? Dad viewed money as a means to an end. It wasn't the finish line. Rather than save every single rupee to buy the biggest house, he'd rather have extra money to spend generously on food and friends and sharing. Live in a house you can afford, but eat like a king.

NEVER WISH YOUR BROTHER DEAD.

My dad never raised his hand to me. Ever. He didn't believe in violence. He did, however, have a temper, something I experienced whenever I misbehaved. One night the whole family was watching a movie together at the house, and there was this scene where this woman grotesquely, repeatedly, and bloodily stabbed some guy. The day before, I just had a fight with my brother about who gets to watch the TV before going to bed—or some other stupid territorial battle that takes place when you share a room with a sibling—so when the woman stabbed the guy, I said under my breath, "God, I wish that was my brother."

My father snapped his entire head toward me, and in the deepest, most furious tone I'd ever heard, roared, "WHAT DID YOU SAY?"

"I, um, I said . . . I wish that was my brother?"

"GET OUT OF THIS ROOM!"

"What, I was just kidding—"

"Kunal, get out of this damn room! If I ever hear you say something like that again, I will kick you out of this FUCKING HOUSE!"

I ran from the room, sobbing. My mom came into my bedroom after me and said that I should never say things about murdering my brother, and that even though I didn't mean it, it's still not a nice thing to say. I nodded, though I thought she was wrong.

The next morning, I woke up for breakfast and my dad was sipping tea at the table, and I felt that he, too, was embarrassed about the night before. We didn't really know how to break the ice. He then turned to me and said calmly, "Kunal, I'm sorry that I screamed at you. I shouldn't have used bad language, but you should never say that, or anything like that, in this house again."*

Sometimes when we are young (and even as adults) we can get caught up in a moment and say things we don't mean. Or maybe in that moment, we do mean them. But I think what Dad was instilling in me was to be responsible for my words. Because words *are* powerful; they can hurt and wound, and one word can lead to a thousand horrors. So don't forget to be impeccable with your words.

Also, don't wish anyone dead.

USE A CUSHION (AND NOT JUST FOR YOUR BUTT).

Every one of Dad's budgets has a category he calls "cushion." He believes that you should enjoy your money, but that you will sleep more soundly if you have just a bit of extra wiggle room. This way, even if things go wrong, you'll still have some margin for error. Having a cushion means always having a Plan B. That's why I

---

* It's a peculiar sensation when your parents apologize to you. It humanizes them. I feel that's the hardest thing about growing up—watching your parents become more and more human.

stuck with my business degree before I got my master's in acting. To have a Plan B. To have a cushion.

YOU CAN HAVE A SOFT DEMEANOR AND NOT BE SOFT.

In the early 1990s, protests broke out between students and police in riot gear over discrimination in the education system, all within walking distance of our home. Our eyes were glued to the TV and the bloodshed it depicted and we often talked about it over dinner.

My dad came home from work early one day. "Kunal, come with me."

He took me to his gun cabinet.

"Help me clean these guns."

We cleaned and loaded every single gun. He was a collector of antique guns and owned seven rifles. He showed me how to double- and triple-check that the safety was on.

"I'm giving you and your brother a key," he told me. "The key to this gun cabinet. If anything happens, open the cabinet, and get ready to defend your home."

I was scared shitless. My father, as always, was a rock. He might speak softly and smile with dimples and patiently discuss both sides of every issue, but when the chips were down and the tide of violence was upon us, this was a man who owned seven rifles and was willing to use them to protect his family.

JUST SHOW UP FOR THEM.

At the dinner table, sometimes we talked about death. *What does it mean to mourn?* In India, when someone close to you dies, you drop everything and you go to their house. You show up to support the family as much as to show respect for the person who has died. You see this in nature, too: if a monkey dies in the forest, the other monkeys congregate and sit in silence.

I was eight when one of my uncles died. It was the first time I can remember knowing someone who had died. On the way to my uncle's house I said, "Dad, I feel scared to see a dead body."

"Kunal, it's okay. In your life you will see a lot of dead bodies. All you have to do is accept death and just show up during the family's time of grief."

"But what do I say? What do I do?"

"You don't have to say anything. By showing up you are reassuring them that they are not alone. Just *being there* is enough."

STAND UP WHEN IT COUNTS.

One night Dad wanted to take us all out to dinner. There was an air of excitement since this restaurant had come highly recommended as the new hot spot in town, and to top it off, it was also my favorite cuisine, Indian-Chinese. Which is basically Chinese food that tastes like curry. A very fat and fancy maître d' seated us at our table and as we waited for the waiter, we mused over the menu. I was damn near drooling looking at the other tables filled with spicy goodness. We waited five minutes for a waiter to arrive...then ten minutes...then fifteen...Nothing. We were being completely ignored by all of the staff.

Then, at an adjacent table, we watched as a white family was brought over and seated. Out of nowhere, three waiters immediately showed up to take their order.

Incensed, my father stood up in the middle of the restaurant and asked loudly, "Where is the manager of this restaurant?"

Fat, fancy maître d' waddled in, mumbling and fumbling.

"What country do we live in?" my dad asked him.

"Excuse me, sir?"

"What. Country. Do. We. Live. In."

"Sir, we live in India."

"Is India a democracy?"

"Yes."

"Then why am I being treated like a third-class citizen in my own country? I have been sitting here for fifteen minutes with my family, not one person has served us, but as soon as a table of foreigners sits down, the entire restaurant shows up to take their order."

Silence. Then Dad says, "Come, children, we are not eating here. We will never come here again." We left. I could see the anger in Dad's eyes, and the shame on the maître d's face.

My father always had a lot of pride, but he also had a sense of proportion. In the infamous Archie's Gallery Valentine's Day Card Showdown, my father didn't think I had truly been wronged, which is why he paid the clerk the price of the card. In the restaurant, he felt like his basic right to be treated without prejudice had been violated. He stood up when it mattered.

That night in the restaurant, it occurred to me that I'm the kind of person who, in a similar situation, might have noticed what was happening but probably would not have done anything about it. I would have quietly devoured every last bite of that Indian-Chinese meal (if and when it was finally delivered), paid the bill, and gone home. Looking back at it now, I wonder if perhaps when my dad was a boy, he saw his dad standing up to some injustice and wondered about his own ability to do the same. Over time he grew into a man and stepped into that role, teaching his children right from wrong. As I write this, I can feel myself changing, maturing, growing into a man, someone who will stand up for everything he believes in. At least, I really hope so.

TREAT A KING AND A BEGGAR THE SAME.

This says it all.

WHEN YOU LEND MONEY, DON'T EXPECT TO GET IT BACK.

This advice was passed down to my father from his father. It's part of living with a big heart. Surround yourself with people that you love. Give freely. Don't expect it back.

GOOD-BYE IS JUST AN OPPORTUNITY FOR HELLO.

When I was eighteen, it was time for me to leave for America. A large crowd of friends and cousins had gathered at the airport to send me on my way, but once I had hugged all of them good-bye and kissed and cried with my mother, and once I had checked all of my luggage, finally, it was just me and my dad.

"I'll walk Kunal to the gate," he said.

The two of us walked all the way to where they collected tickets and you boarded the plane—you could do that back then—not saying much. At the counter he smiled his deep-dimpled smile and charmed the pretty flight attendant, saying, "My son is finally leaving the house to become a man. He's going to America today to study."

"That's lovely, sir," she said. "I have a two-year-old myself. I look forward to the day when I can walk him to the plane as you are doing."

"It's a very proud moment," my father said.

"It is," I mumbled, trying to add something memorable and appropriate and failing miserably.

The flight attendant looked at me. "You know what, Mr. Nayyar, to help you on your journey, I'm going to upgrade you to first class, so you can fly in comfort for your first big trip alone."

Yes!

And finally it was time to say good-bye to my father. We could not put it off any longer. I didn't know how he was going to react, whether he would be heroic and strong, give me a pat on the back and gruffly say something like *You got this*, or if he would dissolve into tears.

"I have something for you," he said instead.

I secretly hoped it was an envelope of money, but he instead pulled out a small book with a green cover: *The Prophet*, by Kahlil Gibran, the Lebanese poet and philosopher.

"Read this book, Kunal. Refer to it whenever you have to answer any of the difficult questions life will ask you."

And then he didn't say good-bye. He didn't say he would miss me. Instead he pulled me in close and said, "I love you, and I believe in you wholeheartedly. You will make a great life for yourself."

Tears began to well up in my eyes (as they do again, even now, as I write this).

He continued. "This is not good-bye, my son. This is many more opportunities to say hello."

We hugged. As I walked to the Jetway, I turned back to look at him one last time. He said, "Kunal, when you've settled in on the flight, turn to the chapter on children."

I waved again, boarded the plane, and immediately tore the book open and read the chapter on children. Which is a complete lie, because first I geeked out over my free first-class seat with all the cool buttons and stuff! I had no idea how to work anything. I kept trying to turn on the TV but was instead just pushing the dinner tray open. The Indian businessman next to me, looking relaxed after a swirl of very important meetings, I presumed, was working his TV just fine. I figured he probably thought that having an overexcitable nitwit next to him would ruin his journey in first class. He probably hated me. He was probably about to demand a seat change for one of us. I was going to get demoted back to coach before takeoff.

"Hey, son, let me show you how to do that," he said. I noticed his sleek reading glasses and his gentle face.

Okay. This is all going to work out okay.

I sank into my leather easy chair and began to peruse many of the astounding number of horrible movies that are available on airplanes. I believe my first choice of the evening was *Tarzan*. Hours later, unable to sleep, I finally opened *The Prophet* and turned to the chapter on children.

ON CHILDREN

And a woman who held a babe against her bosom said, "Speak to us of Children." And he said:

Your children are not your children.

They are the sons and daughters of Life's longing for itself.

They come through you but not from you,

And though they are with you, yet they belong not to you.

You may give them your love but not your thoughts.

For they have their own thoughts.

You may house their bodies but not their souls,

For their souls dwell in the house of tomorrow, which you cannot visit, not even in your dreams.

You may strive to be like them, but seek not to make them like you.

For life goes not backward nor tarries with yesterday.

You are the bows from which your children as living arrows are sent forth.

The archer sees the mark upon the path of the infinite, and He bends you with His might that His arrows may go swift and far.

Let your bending in the archer's hand be for gladness;

For even as he loves the arrow that flies, so He loves also the bow that is stable.

Dziko and Me

I SHOWED UP TO COLLEGE A FEW DAYS EARLIER THAN MOST of my classmates. There was an additional orientation specifically for international students before the rest of the local students showed up, so the dorms were almost completely empty. This was 1999, my freshman year at the University of Portland, and I had just arrived from India. I really had no idea what to expect of college, except what I had seen in the movie *American Pie*. You know, the movie where everyone's getting laid? Yeah, this was not like that. The resident assistant, a friendly chap with bright blue eyes called Kaiden (great name), showed me to my room, gave me some paperwork to fill out, closed the door, and left.

I stared at the bunk beds and the barren walls and the gray carpet and suddenly realized I was absolutely alone. It was finally sinking in that I was eight thousand miles away from home. That I didn't know anyone. I looked at the empty room and realized that I didn't even know what to do for the next ten minutes—should I unpack, brush my teeth, wash my face, take a quick nap, fill out Kaiden's forms?

Aimless, I headed downstairs to explore the campus. I found Kaiden talking to an enormous black guy sitting on the floor with his legs crossed Indian-style.* He looked like a giant kid as he sat there twirling his giant dreadlocks. Even sitting down, he appeared to be three times my size.

"This is Dziko; he's from France," Kaiden told me.

Dziko smiled. One of those smiles like a baby, the ones that force you to smile along, too, because it comes from a place of pure happiness. This was Dziko's smile. Everything about him was serene.

Then he stood up.

Dziko rose and kept rising, until it seemed like he would block out the sun. I was awestruck and made the dumb joke that I'm sure every human being had told him his entire life: "Wow, you're so tall. Do you play basketball?"

"No," he mumbled in a gentle French accent. *Sarcasm?* I thought. Then he smiled and nodded his head. He was making a joke. He, in fact, did play basketball, and at six foot ten with the dreadlocks—he would be our school's starting power forward. He was 250 pounds of pure, ripped muscle. A giant with the face of an innocent child.

"This is your new roommate, Kunal," said Kaiden.

Roommate? Did I hear that correctly? In that tiny dorm room? Do I get top bunk or bottom? I was both excited and terrified, and probably a little jet-lagged. Kaiden pointed us in the direction of the international students' orientation and we strolled off together, him in shorts and flip-flops, me in my long-sleeve shirt and corduroy pants, and I could tell right away that we were going to become friends. The rapport was instant. Or at least I thought so, because I basically spent the next several hours just asking him

---

* Or, what we just call "sitting."

questions about basketball.* He patiently answered in his French accent—I later learned he spoke five languages—and even though he was a man of few words, his calm demeanor and kind smile told me, *This is okay; he's also far away from home, you need each other, you've found a friend, this new life can work.*

❖

Our dorm room smelled like the East. Dziko was a devout Muslim and said his prayers every morning, so between my incense and his herbs and tonics, there was this heavy dose of India and East Africa with a subtle hint of beeswax (for his dreads, I think). We spent a lot of time in that little room. He didn't drink or party and at the time neither did I, so we'd come home from class and basically watch movies, drink Coca-Cola, and scarf down boxes of Pringles. We played guitar together. We scanned the campus looking for pretty girls, spending far more time looking for them than talking to them.

Dziko was an eater. At the cafeteria he loaded up two trays of food and a third just for drinks. He only had two hands, which meant that I also had to carry two trays—one tray with my little lunch, and one tray full of Dziko's drinks—water, milk, Diet Coke, Mountain Dew, and orange juice as a chaser. (Dziko unintentionally helped me learn how to be a waiter that year.) And in the time it took me to eat my bowl of pasta, he somehow devoured chicken, ribs, and a corned beef sandwich. Seemingly all in one bite. Ten minutes later he'd dash off for six hours of basketball practice, and

---

* I haven't mentioned that one of my dreams was to play in the NBA. I was religious about Michael Jordan, and my American cousins would send me tapes of the Chicago Bulls' games. If badminton hadn't panned out, I was going to try my hand at the Indian Basketball League.

to this day it still astonishes me that he did all that eating and working out without once vomiting.

We became notorious around campus as a sort of odd couple. Dziko was more hippie than cool—I mean "cool" in the traditional sense of frat-boy cool—but since he played basketball he had instant street cred. And he could *play.* Duke University once played us in the Rose Garden in Portland. I had a front-row seat to cheer him on, watching as he ripped down an offensive rebound and then dunked on future NBA player Shane Battier. (I later tracked down the video and framed the dunk, giving him the photo as a birthday present.) When we walked around he slapped high fives with other athletes that I would befriend, too. If someone needed to find me they asked Dziko, and if someone needed to find Dziko, well . . . they could just, you know, *see* him.

Dziko helped me deal with some of the culture shocks associated with being foreign. Even if most of the adjustments were subtle. Take cooking. After years of having all the mango milk shakes and butter chicken I could eat prepared for me at home, I wasn't exactly what you would call an Iron Chef, or a chef at all. One night I was studying in the dorm with some guys from my marketing class, and one of them said, "Dude, I'm starving. Let's make some ramen."

I had a vague knowledge of ramen, as we eat those noodles in India, the Maggi brand. But I had no idea how they were made. Is it even *possible* to cook them yourself? Can that be done? Like in a microwave? Or do we need cooking oil and stuff? I followed the guys to the community kitchen and watched as they pulled out saucepans and filled them with water. I had no frigging clue what to do.

"Kunal?"

"Just give me a sec."

I stared at the stove and marveled that my friends knew how to operate such a complicated apparatus.

"I'm not hungry," I said, unable to tell them that I didn't know how to boil water, and not even sure that they were in fact boiling water. That was a rare white lie, as I was so thoroughly earnest and determined to play things by the book. For example, during freshman orientation, they gave us the standard lecture about how students were not allowed to have guns or carry weapons or build bombs or whatever. Obvious stuff. But instead of just nodding like the rest of the crowd I thought, *No weapons. Wait. WAIT.* As a gift, my brother had given me this beautiful hand-carved pocketknife.

I raised my hand. "What about a knife?"

"What do you mean?"

"I have a really big knife. I just wanted to declare it to all of you."

The other students looked at me, maybe a little alarmed, although this was pre-9/11 so maybe not so much. They would, however, be alarmed if they knew about the sheets on my bed. Since I was so accustomed to someone taking care of the laundry back home, I had this misunderstanding that somehow, perhaps while I was at class, our bedsheets were being laundered for us at least once a week. Apparently this wasn't the case. I slept in the same sheets for eleven months without them ever being washed.

Living in the dorm was weird for me because I was very uncomfortable using the public showers. In India, you rarely see exposed skin unless you're lucky enough to see *all* the skin, if you know what I mean. We usually keep our bodies covered. So I would enter the showers fully clothed, head to toe, while the other guys walked around completely naked, balls and all, and I would derobe *inside* the shower. I even timed my trips to the bathroom at odd hours just to avoid the awkwardness; I was that weird kid from India who took showers at three in the morning.

The biggest awkwardness, of course, came in my communications with the opposite sex. In the very beginning, the first several months, Dziko and I didn't flirt with girls at all. He was a devout Muslim and took pains to orient himself away from sin. And me? Well, I was basically useless. I mean, I remember at one party with Dziko I literally asked a girl, "Do you want to do a slow dance with me?" I was still twelve years old when it came to knowing how to talk to women.

Yet somehow, I lived in the illusion that every girl I saw was in love with me. All it took was for someone to glance in my general vicinity. I was accustomed to the slower-paced dating game in New Delhi, where a courtship takes weeks or months and you do the A-to-Zs of going on movie dates, hoping to hold hands in the popcorn.* In America? Girls would often hug me and walk arm in arm with me and stuff, and then when I'd try to kiss them they'd say, "Ew, Kunal, you're like my brother!"

So, yes, freshman year, Dziko and I missed out on the scenes of *Animal House*–like parties and fratty debauchery, but the truth is we weren't all that sad about it. We made up for it in other ways. He taught me French pop songs like the hit "Je t'aime," and I memorized all the lyrics in French even though I didn't know what they meant. For our school's "International Night" we threw together a makeshift band—we even had a guy who played the bongos—and did a group number of the song "La Bamba." Dziko strummed his guitar and wore an African hat—smiling his baby smile—and I wore a

---

* See letters H and I in "My A-to-Z Guide for Getting Nookie in New Delhi During High School," page 17.

bandana with the Indian flag on it. The entire crowd of twelve ate it up and cheered us on, and for one night we were rock stars.

❖

I came home to the dorm one night to find Dziko in bed.

"D, why are you asleep? It's only nine thirty."

He looked like he was stoned, but I knew that wasn't the case because Dziko didn't do drugs or drink alcohol.

"I'm drunk," Dziko said, clearly pleased with himself.

"You're drunk?"

"No more of this religion stuff." He laughed. "I'm done."

Okay, then. Just like that. Everything changed. Dziko and I began a new chapter of our college life. To this day I don't know exactly why he gave up religion, but I do know that when he changed his mind, suddenly, *it was on.* Since Dziko gave himself permission to drink alcohol, now I, too, could push my boundaries. He was my compass. It was time to fully throw ourselves into the wild, wild West.*

But . . . how? We didn't know much about drinking or partying. The only parties we knew about were thrown by Dziko's athlete friends, so imagine all those tall, buff, Adonis-looking jocks and these beautiful, hot girls in miniskirts . . . and me. All these cool people were listening to hip-hop and doing keg stands, and I'd show up in my oversize baggy T-shirt and long hair. I looked like a cross between a hippie and a slum dweller who somehow spoke impeccable English. I just didn't fit in.

Through some trial and error, I realized that regular college parties weren't really for me. I didn't want to get drunk there. So instead I took advantage of school holidays like Thanksgiving,

---

* I'm not sure I got that reference right.

Christmas, and spring break, when I knew that almost no one would be on campus. In those quiet weeks Dziko and I would throw our own little versions of a dorm party, where there were just a half dozen people sitting around drinking Bacardi Breezers, and with any luck there would be a girl I could make out with.

Sometimes Dziko and I just went to the all-night coffee shop, playing chess, strumming guitars, swapping life stories until the early morning hours. He rarely spoke about his family or background, but as the months rolled by I learned that childhood had been a traumatic and difficult time for him. Maybe that's what that ever-present smile was hiding. His father was a human rights activist in Mauritania, North Africa, and one day, when Dziko was ten, his father didn't come home. He had been extradited to Paris, where there was a warrant for his arrest, and they didn't see him again for two years. Dziko grew up in the shadow of persecution, imprisonment, or worse every day.

But I felt safe with Dziko. When I was with this gentle giant, no one could touch me. Years later, when we were in Paris together, we were getting some late-night street food and a few thuggy-looking kids surrounded me with an aggressive look in their eyes. Next thing I knew Dziko was standing over them and calmly saying something to them in French. Within three seconds they were gone. He really was my rock.

He was also, briefly, my bedmate. Let me explain. In the summer between our freshman and sophomore years, the two of us lived in a house with five girls from the track team. He was friendly with them because of the sports thing and had heard they were looking for a roommate, or in this case, roommates. It was a six-bedroom house and each girl had her own room, so Dziko and I shared a room to save money. And the only place to sleep in the room was on a futon.

Soon Dziko was kissing girls. This shouldn't have surprised me, as when you're six ten with .0000001 percent body fat, girls tend to notice you. Dziko had met these two inseparable Japanese girls, Yasu and Arisu, and I realized that he had leveled up in the video game of life.

"So you're having sex with Arisu?"

He just smiled his baby smile.

"What's it like?"

"None of your business."

"I mean, come on, she's like five foot three."

He brushed it off. "Now you and Yasu—you and her, nice."

"What do you mean 'nice'? You want me to get with her? I don't even know her."

"She'll have sex with you," Dziko said.

"What? Stop screwing with me."

"She'll do it."

"What if I try something and she says no?"

"She won't. She told Arisu she thinks you're cute."

So Dziko concocted this evil plan to get me laid: We'd invite the two of them over to the house, and then he would depart with Arisu, leaving me alone with Yasu. I was so nervous. Not only was I a virgin; we didn't even speak the same language. I did a condom check, worried that I would put it on inside out.

The big night comes and D gives me a fist bump and a wink, and then takes off with Arisu. Yasu was very much cool with what was going on. Without much discussion we headed to the futon, switched off the lights, and proceeded to do what college students do. And a second time. And a third time.*

---

* That's what happens when you're a rookie.

The next morning I woke up and looked Yasu in the eye. She looked so peaceful. I said, "Good morning, Arisu."*

"WHAT?" she said.

"I said, 'Good morning, Yasu.'"

"You said 'Arisu'!"

"No no no, I'm just still asleep, I'm mumbling. I said 'Yasu.'"

For some reason she got really mad. *Women.* Believe it or not, Yasu and I didn't make it as a couple, and come to think of it, neither did Arisu and Dziko. Arisu became super-psycho, showing up everywhere we went; she even started popping out of bushes to spook us. I would go with Dziko to basketball practice and watch him shoot free throws—ten in a row, *swish* . . . thirty in a row, *swish* . . . and when he had *swished* forty-nine consecutive free throws, just before fifty, I would wave and yell out to no one, "Hey, what's up, Arisu!"

Clank.

❖

Dziko once helped me become the next Mark Zuckerberg. I had a marketing assignment for sales class, and I had to start a new business that would actually make some cash. My idea was to come up with a matchmaking service that would let people find dates for the university dance. I called the service "Cupid."

For the very competitive price of two dollars, people would fill out a questionnaire and submit a photo, and I would use a mathematical algorithm to match the guys and the girls. (The methodology behind my algorithm: I just picked a girl's questionnaire and stapled it to a guy's questionnaire, more or less at

---

* Right. Her name is not Arisu.

random.) But how do you find the customers? Who would pay two dollars for a match? Who would trust Cupid? This was still several years before Facebook, so Dziko and I literally had to go door-to-door in the girls' dorm. We headed over just after 7 p.m., figuring they would have all finished dinner but not yet be asleep or out doing whatever girls did on a school night.

"Do you have a boyfriend?" I asked each girl as she answered the door. If she said yes, I didn't waste any time, just said thank you and knocked on the next door. Dziko didn't say a word. He was loving every moment of this.

In a sense, this was a precursor of what the online dating business would later become—a means of making money from the gathering of information from people based on unlikely promises of an intimate connection. We visited 679 girls' rooms, and I'm proud to say a full twenty-four women signed up for Cupid. Matching them to twenty-four guys was the easy part; I just walked down my hall. I made seventy-three dollars in profit and received a B. I know the math doesn't make sense, but I had to pay Dziko 25 percent because he was a junior partner in my venture. (The winning company was a German bratwurst stand that raked in thousands of dollars a week; the dean had to shut it down because it siphoned off too much revenue from the school cafeteria.)

Obviously, Cupid was just ahead of its time.

❖

At the end of our sophomore year our basketball coach was let go. I didn't think much about this at the time, but then one day at lunch Dziko said, "Kunal, the coach is gone."

"Okay."

"I think I want to follow him."

"Okay . . . I mean. Wait. What does that mean?"

"I want to play basketball at another school."

"Um, that's cool," I said, masking my anxiety. "I'll support whatever you want to do."

The next few days were a blur. We caught wind of other players leaving and transferring to other colleges, and soon Dziko, too, was receiving offers from other schools. It wasn't sinking in. *Can you really transfer as a junior?* Dziko wouldn't leave. He couldn't leave. Why would he leave?

The next day he came into our room, elated, looking as happy as I had ever seen him. "I got transferred! I'm going to Cal Poly!"

"That's awesome," I lied.

"I'm going to live near the beach, Kunal!"

My heart dropped.

It happened so quickly. The semester was winding down and we were packing up the room and peeling off posters and memories from the wall. I was about to head back to India for the summer.

We only had a few days left together, and we both knew it, and we both must have thought about it, but neither of us said much of anything. We didn't know how to say good-bye. We did our usual things. We didn't talk about the future or the past. We watched a few movies and played some chess.

But you can't run away from the inevitable, no matter how hard you try. Good-byes happen, but so do hellos. It was time to say good-bye. I zipped up my bags and checked to make sure I had my toothbrush (an odd observation given the gravity of the situation). Dziko was sitting on the bed, his legs crossed Indian-style,* twirling his dreadlocks.

I looked at him, not sure what to say.

He helped me with my bag and gave me a hug. "I love you, man."

I told him I loved him. We hugged again, clapped each other on the back, and that was that.

I called my mother that night from the airport and said that Dziko was leaving, and before I could even get the words out the tears began to stream down my face. I broke down and wept. I felt empty. I missed him already.

"Why are you crying, Kunal?"

She didn't understand. And I didn't have the words to explain it to her. My relationship with Dziko was in some ways more intimate than anything I had experienced with women at that point. There wasn't the sex to get in the way. We shared the deepest and most sensitive memories of our pasts. No one knew me like he did. And now he was gone.

I remained Dziko's biggest fan. Two years later, I was at a theater party and Cal Poly was playing Duke in the conference finals; if they won they would earn a bid to March Madness. The TV was on mute and I watched it by myself, ignoring the rest of the party, cheering every time Dziko touched the ball. The game was close and with just seconds left on the clock, Cal Poly was down by three.

"Give D the ball! Give him the ball!" I screamed at the mute TV.

Dziko posted up and they did give him the ball. For some reason Duke doubled him (honestly, this didn't make much sense) and D made the right play, passing the ball to his wide-open teammate

---

* Again, just sitting.

for a three. The ball went up in a rainbow, the buzzer sounded, up, up, up . . . and clank. It just missed the target. Cal Poly lost.

After college he tried to play in Germany, but developed chronic foot problems and never quite made it to the European League. But the truth is, I don't think D ever loved basketball. He cared more for playing guitar, conversation, wine, flowers, and sitting on the beach. He loved the outdoors and good people. Sometimes I'll think about that smile, and it'll brighten up my day.

We stayed in touch, of course, and we still remain very close friends. Years after we both graduated I would travel to Paris with him for his sister's wedding, and finally I met the family I had heard so much about. I remember doing shots with his ninety-year-old grandmother, Babushka, who carried around a flask of vodka. I met his father, who had been a political refugee. And his Russian mother, who worked as an accountant at Euro Disney. I learnt about their struggles and their triumphs and the eventual reunion of the entire family in Paris after so many lost years. And on the night of his sister's wedding, on a boat floating down the Seine, we stared at the twinkling dark water as an elderly pianist from New Orleans plucked out blues notes and belted,

When the night has gone, and the land is dark,
And the moon is the only light we'll see.

"Stand by Me." In French, no less.

The Art of the Head Bobble

LET'S TAKE A SECOND AND TALK ABOUT THE INDIAN HEAD bobble. Yes, I am going to go there. Because yes, it's true that Indians bobble their heads all the time. That's not a racist thing to say because a) I am Indian, and b) bobbling our heads is a very important and sophisticated form of communication. When you bobble your head you're not really saying yes, and you're not really saying no. So much is communicated and so much is not communicated by the bobble. It could mean:

I'm full.

I'm hungry.

I'm confused.

I'm happy.

I understand.

Talk to me.

Stop talking.

Never talk to me again.

So how does one decipher the bobble? The truth is, you can't. There aren't any bobble variations or inflections, and this one universal head bobble works greatly to our advantage. Imagine you're trying to buy something from me and you say, "Ten rupees."

I bobble my head.

"Twenty rupees."

I bobble my head.

"Thirty rupees?"

And so on. I ripped you off for twenty rupees just by bobbling my head. Greatest invention ever. I wonder if the bobble was born from when we were oppressed by the British. Maybe it was just the safest way to avoid getting beaten.

Subconsciously, I suppose I do the bobble all the time, but I really unleash it when I want to use my Indianness in my favor. For example, if I see a lovely woman and want to stand out from the crowd, I will stand in her vicinity and bobble the shit out of my head and use a thicker accent. She'll be charmed by my exoticness, she'll want to know where I'm from, we'll chat, and she'll think, *This guy's harmless, he's Indian! And his head bobble is so cute.*

Garbage, Man

LIKE EVERY COLLEGE STUDENT, I NEEDED A JOB FOR SOME extra cash. Problem was, I didn't have any "job qualifications," because, to be honest, I had never worked a day in my life. So the summer after my freshman year, I decided to take a job in the university's housekeeping department (because the job description exactly matched my level of expertise). My job was to clean toilets, empty out the Dumpsters, scrub the floors, move furniture, set up chairs for events, and basically do everything else that no one else in the university wanted to do.

Aaaaaaand I loved it. I swear. I took pride in my ability to stack and unstack chairs. Not to brag, guys, but I might actually be the fastest chair stacker this side of the equator. I figured out a superbly efficient way of folding the chair's legs in one fluid motion; it must have been muscle memory from all my years of badminton.

My boss, Luis, looked a bit like the villain from God of War. Or like the genie in *Aladdin* if he was Satan and Medusa's love child. He had a very black and pointed goatee, a sharp, hooked nose, a long, skinny tongue that he loved to show off, and a scar down the middle of his chest from triple bypass open-heart surgery. He claimed to have slept with thousands of women and seemed determined to tell us about each and every one. He also would do this weird tongue thing, where he would show us the strength of his tongue by picking up M&Ms off the table without his teeth or lips. It was the most disgusting and yet most fascinating thing I had ever seen. He also drove a red Corvette, which automatically made him very, very cool. There's cool, and then there's Luis cool.

Every morning Luis would give me a new objective for the day, such as: "A professor just died. Go clean out his office." Not even twenty-four hours after this poor soul had lost his life, I was in his office, packing up his possessions, clearing out all the books and the plants and the memories, and somehow trying to squeeze his couch and table out the office door. It was my first lesson in physics, really; *just because you can get something into the room doesn't mean you can get it out.* I spent four hours cleaning that office, and another four trying to squeeze the furniture out the door. *Maybe this is what it feels like to give birth.*

Another morning Luis would say, "Empty out the women's dormitory Dumpster!" So I hopped into my little truck and drove to the girls' dorm, and scraped the Dumpster walls of gunk. I don't need to tell you what I found in the Dumpster, right? Let's just say that I discovered a new appreciation for people who tie their garbage bags up tightly, because there is nothing worse than actually having to touch, see, and smell what people are throwing away. So tie up your garbage bags tightly, please!

One member of my daily cohort was this guy whose name was Khrish. He always smelled like fish. He secretly wanted to be a Nepalese pop star, and would always sing us these terrible songs about his love for mountains. Everyone teased poor Khrish about his singing, but he didn't mind. Because he didn't understand that they were laughing at him.

"Cover your ears, Khrish is at it again!" "Run for shelter, here comes the Khrish train!"

Khrish would laugh and keep going.

"STOP THE GODDAMN SINGING!"

And Khrish would raise his voice and belt the tune as loudly as he could. On top of his vocal challenges—that is, hitting a single note on key—Khrish faced an uphill battle, given that he wanted to be a Nepalese pop star who sings Nepalese songs about the Himalayas . . . in Portland.

I loved those guys. You probably imagine the housekeeping department as a group of people who clean up other people's messes for money and don't really want to be there, but in my experience that wasn't true. We all had fun together. We took pride in our work. It didn't feel like a *lowly job* or a *bad job;* it just felt like a job. And it also taught me a lesson or two about cultural sensitivities, and how race relations can be a two-way street. One day I was joking around with a coworker named Andy, a chubby ex-marine with a soft demeanor. Andy lit up when I told him my mother was coming to Portland for a visit.

"You bringing her to the company picnic?" Andy asked.

"I don't know if she'll get along with all the white trash," I said.

Andy didn't say much later that afternoon. Or the next few days. At the time I didn't really understand the full connotations behind "white trash," and I didn't know it was derogatory. I suppose, in hindsight, a phrase that uses the word *trash* can't really be seen as a compliment, but I thought I was just making a joke. A few days later Andy still wasn't talking to me, so I asked him if something was wrong.

"Kunal, don't you know that I'm white trash, too? Why would you call us that?"

"I'm sorry," I said, meaning it. "I didn't really know what it meant." And that was the truth. I sincerely didn't know that *white trash* was a horrible term. I explained this in great detail to Andy, and he realized that I didn't have any negative feelings about him, or about our coworkers, or about white people in general, and soon we were back to being chums again. But it reminded me that words can be hurtful.

Lunch was every day's highlight. We had an hour break and everyone shared their food on a big communal table, usually while laughing at the sheer volume of hygiene products we'd found in the morning's trash; or Khrish's latest song; or details from Cool Luis's disgusting orgies. Someone always brought fish, others pasta, some brought chicken salad; I always brought peanut butter and jelly sandwiches because it was the only thing I knew how to make.

As the summer drew to a close, on one of my last days on the job, I had to drive the mini-truck to the computer lab, where I was told to pick up a desk. Easy enough. I drove the truck up a long ramp, parked it on the landing in the front of the building, and went inside to help the guys lift the desk.

Then I heard screaming.

I ran outside.

The mini-truck was rolling backward. Down the ramp. With no one in it.

At the bottom of this ramp is the main university lawn, the kind of picnic area that they show in every college brochure where students are reading and playing Frisbee and sunbathing. The truck careened straight toward this lawn, and before I could make a move, the truck hit the bottom of the ramp, toppled upside down in the picnic area, and flipped on its belly.

Oh man.

In my hurry to grab the desk I had forgotten to set the emergency brake, and the truck simply glided back down the ramp.

Out of nowhere—somehow within seconds—a man came sprinting toward the scene, barking into a walkie-talkie. A short, stocky guy. Looked like a God of War villain. It was Luis. My boss.

"Is anyone hurt?" Luis asked.

"No."

"Any damage?"

No damage. Luis immediately took command of the scene. He set the place in order and right there I saw why my boss was *the* boss.

In that moment, of course, I was worried about the truck and anyone on the lawn who might be hurt, but later, when the guilt began to creep into the pit of my stomach, I worried this would cause problems with the university and/or jeopardize my scholarship. What if this incident cost me everything that my family had invested? Life doesn't just fuck you over on a Saturday night when you're blackout drunk; it can just as easily fuck you over on a Tuesday afternoon when you're going to lift a desk.

But Luis took the fall. He wouldn't tell the department which one of his guys had made the mistake and, as a result, he was suspended for two weeks without pay.

"That's not right," I said. "It should be my punishment."

Luis wouldn't listen to me.

I felt awful. "Please. It's my fault. Fire me. I'll fire myself. I'm fired." I still feel awful. I pleaded for him to let me take the blame, but no matter what I said, he wouldn't budge. He insisted on being my fall guy.

I suppose we all had each other's backs. We all screwed around and we told dirty jokes and we laughed at each other's expense, and maybe we all came from different walks of life and places of origin—immigrants, marines, Nepal, Texas, India—but at the end of the day it didn't matter. At the end of the day we stuck together. We had an unspoken bond; together we were safe.

Many years later, my wife and I endowed a scholarship at the University of Portland. For the inauguration of the fund I came to the school auditorium to give a little speech to the students. There were about three hundred people in the room.

In the back of the auditorium, someone raised his hand. An older guy.

"You won't remember me, but we worked together once," the man said.

It was Khrish.

We ran toward each other with open arms. It felt like the movies. We hugged in the center of the stage as the crowd erupted in applause.

Later that night we met for beers and swapped life stories. Nothing much had changed in his life. Except for one thing.

He had a new song.

And you know what?

It wasn't bad. It was actually, dare I say it, decent.

And this time no one laughed.

Holiday Traditions Part 2: Dussehra

Dussehra (*du-SHAR-uh*): *n.* annual Hindu festival taking place in the fall, celebrating the victory of good over evil.

DUSSEHRA IS MY FAVORITE INDIAN FESTIVAL BECAUSE, WHEN I was a kid, at night our family would walk to the nearest public park, where a crowd of a thousand people would watch, spellbound, the burning of a one-hundred-foot, ten-headed demon. The burning of this demon commemorates the victory of King Rama over the demon lord Ravana. Since this occurs near the beginning of the harvest season, some also believe that the religious rituals help to reactivate the vigor and fertility of the soil. Which is great and all. But did I mention the demon was huge and had ten heads and we got to watch it go up in flames? *Kick. Ass.*

Dussehra also has a carnival where you wander from stall to stall, buy snacks (not beef, obviously), and waste your rupees on games like shooting water balloons and such. One year when I was about eleven years old, I was asked to volunteer at one of these stalls.

These are the rules of the exciting game at my stall: for two rupees, you throw a penny in a bucket full of water, and then you have five seconds to dip your hand in the bucket and try to find your penny. Wooo-hooooo, right?! Who *wouldn't* want to play this game? My job was to advertise this game to the passersby.

"Try the water bucket!" I yelled. "Get your hands wet! Win a prize!"

When people ignored me I screamed louder. "THROW A PENNY! WATER BUCKET! GET YOUR HANDS WET!"

At the end of the night, the stall owner was pleased with the results—and she even gave me twenty rupees. But I'd yelled so much that I'd lost my voice and couldn't even cheer when they burned the demon.

"Here, gargle this," my mother said, handing me a glass of warm water with salt when I got home.

My voice instantly returned. To this day, whenever I lose my voice during a recording session or a play, I still use the remedy of gargling warm water and salt, and I think of pennies and water buckets and ten-headed demons.

> **Dussehra** (*du-SHAR-uh*): ***n.*** 1. annual Hindu festival taking place in the fall, celebrating the victory of good over evil.
> 2. *Game of Thrones* (Real Life Edition). Aka Best. Night. Ever.

The Forbidden Kiss

HER NAME WAS JOYCELL HAYDEN. LOVELY NAME. THE KIND of name belonging to a girl who deserved to be kissed by a prince. And that prince was me. At least, that's the way I would cast the movie. She had pixie-cut blond hair, a round, golden face, and a bounce in her step. We were in Psychology 101 together. She was always first to raise her hand to answer questions and she never had any sweat stains under her arms. I could smell her from seven rows away, strawberries and cream with a touch of black pepper. And the sound of her voice was a sweet, soft melody. It was like she was always half speaking and half singing.

I didn't know how to go about kissing her. It wasn't as easy as running up to her and planting one on her lips, or asking her for a kiss over coffee, or sneak-smooching her while going for her cheek. This kiss had to be planned meticulously. I had a few ideas running around in my head—playing guitar for her in the moonlight, sitting outdoors on a cold night so she'd snuggle next to me for warmth, sharing a milk shake with one straw. Problem was, she barely even knew my name. We had said hello a few times entering or leaving class but had never really even had a conversation.

And then, just like in the movies, an opportunity presented

itself. It was during Thanksgiving week. I obviously stayed at the school; since we only had a week off, it would have been madness to fly back to India. Plus I thought it would be a good time to soak up classic American familial culture. Secretly, though, I hoped there would be a plethora of lonely beauties looking for companionship. One in particular. The university had planned a turkey dinner for all the students who couldn't leave campus, and one day when I was "casually" hovering in her presence, I'd overheard her telling a classmate she wasn't going home for Thanksgiving. Joycell was going to having Thanksgiving dinner at the university? How convenient! We were all to be seated at this really long table. I had been standing close enough (but not too close) to figure out where Joycell would sit. The plan was to fake-pull-out the chair she was going to sit in, pretend I was going to sit in it, and then offer her the seat, pretending to be both chivalrous and adorable at the same time.

When I saw her heading toward her seat I stealthily slid into position. But before I could reach the chair, I tripped over my feet, and instead of pulling the chair out, I had to use it to break my fall. This, however, worked to my advantage. She saw me stumble a bit and it made her giggle. She even offered me a seat next to her, which I gratefully accepted, of course. Apparently tripping and falling is funny in any culture. Finally we were sitting next to each other. Before the meal we had to say a prayer.

"Bless us, O Lord, and these Thy gifts, which we are about to receive, from Thy bounty, through Christ, our Lord. Amen."

We all held hands; her hands were clammy, but I didn't care. I would have held her hands even if they were soaked in pee. I was amazed at the smell of rosemary emanating from her hair. Actually, everything smelled like rosemary. When the food came

I made some joke about how turkey tasted like rotting chicken, which made everyone around me laugh, though I'm not sure they understood English. Truth is, I really just don't like the taste of turkey. Other than Thanksgiving or on a sandwich, does anyone really eat turkey? Over dinner Joycell told me that she couldn't make it home to Utah because of a lack of funds.

"Things happen for a reason," I said, trying to be supportive and secretly making my move. "If you want company, do you wanna hang out after dinner?"

"Yes." No hesitation at all in her reply.

"Your place or mine?" I joked, testing the waters.

She laughed, but I'm not sure she understood the connotation. I suggested we watch a movie, *Ghost*—genius!—and she invited me to watch it in her room. Everything was falling into place. I was so excited I almost couldn't sit still. When the apple pie came I ate it so fast that I almost blacked out from the sugar rush. I didn't even wait for everyone to finish before I was saying the quickest good-byes of my life. I would have run to my room if I hadn't felt like barfing from all the turkey and anxiety playing nookie in my stomach. I picked up the DVD, applied some deodorant to my armpits, and skipped back to her dorm.

Her room smelled like cinnamon and sugar. Like a candle you get on sale at Target. There were family photographs everywhere. She had a very large family, it seemed. It was dimly lit and cozy. Strangely quiet.

"Thanks for inviting me over," I said, then pointed at the candle. "Indians don't usually like cinnamon because we are not exposed to the scent much. But this candle smells divine." I was lying. It smelled awful to me. We both were nervous. We put the movie in and as the opening credits rolled she settled on the floor, with her back resting against the foot of her bed. I sat above her on the edge of the bed. I was trying to play it cool. Didn't want to come off too desperate.

She asked me to join her on the floor. I asked for a cushion; I was skinny and was familiar with butt-bruise syndrome. I settled in next to her. For the second time that night we were sitting side by side.

During the movie our elbows were touching. Her knees were facing me, which I once read in *Cosmopolitan* was a good sign. Anytime you're at a bar and a girl has her knees facing toward you, she wants you. Problem was, we sat there, stuck like that the whole long-ass movie, and no one made a move. Not when Patrick Swayze lifted the coin with his finger, scraping it against the wall. Not when Whoopi Goldberg first made contact with the ghost; not even during the clay-spinning scene when all the mud and clay ends up on Demi Moore's naked body. Nothing happened. But her knees were pointing toward me! *Stupid article.*

The movie was coming to an end, and it seemed, too, that my window of kissy-kissy time was quickly closing. I had to move to Plan B.

"Do you want to listen to the soundtrack?" Conveniently I had the movie soundtrack CD in my pocket. (*Genius!*) I played "Unchained Melody" and told her it was my favorite song of all time. Truth is, that song traumatized me. I did love it once. I loved it so much that I sang it in a high school singing competition. Problem was, the high part was too high for me, so when it came I dropped an entire octave and sang it in a deep voice. The students laughed and laughed. To my credit I did come in third place . . . out of three contestants. I told Joycell none of this. I made up some stuff about how it got me through tough times. I kept using phrases like *silky vocals* and *smooth lyrics*, hoping word association would work on softening her up. When the high part came I sang along in a deep, off-key baritone. This made her giggle. She had a lovely giggle. Cute, shy, and sexy all at once.

I saw an opening. "Would you like to do a slow dance?" I asked. It wasn't even correct English. She obliged. I took her hand and pulled her in close. I could feel her heart throbbing; sweat had collected on her upper lip. This was the moment. I made the move. I leaned in and kissed her lips softly. She hesitated at first, but then she slowly kissed me back. Our lips were locked. She was a good kisser. Aggressive when there was a lull, passive when the moment overheated. I trailed my fingers down her lower back. She tensed up, I apologized, and I told her I would take it slow. I went back to kissing her lips. I kissed her cheek, making my way to her earlobes. She wasn't resisting. I nibbled on the bottom of her ear. She let out a little moan. I continued to her neck and suddenly she tensed up again and pulled away. She sat down on the bed, her cheeks flushed; she turned her face away and began to cry.

"Was it that bad?" I said as a dumb joke. This time she didn't giggle. I kept apologizing. She kept crying. I stood there, not knowing whether to sit, or stand, or leave. And then she said, and I'll never forget it till my dying day, "But you're a Hindu."

Now, a few thoughts crossed my mind. Was she asking me? Was she telling me? Did she not know? Was she doing research for a paper? Did my mouth taste like cumin? Confused, I muttered, "Yes, yes, I am, I am a Hindu." Almost reaffirming to myself that I hadn't changed religion.

"But I'm a Mormon," she said.

I didn't really know what that was, but I guessed it was a religion. Either way it was clear she didn't dig the interreligion saliva swap-fest that just occurred.

"My parents would not be happy with me," she said. "They warned me about becoming this kind of girl."

"But nothing happened; we just kissed," I said.

"I know, but you're not even Christian."

Picture this: A Mormon girl sitting on the edge of her bed. Silent. Tears flowing gently down her cheeks. A Hindu boy standing aimless in the middle of the room. Erect. A forbidden kiss transpired only moments before. "Unchained Melody" in the background. On repeat. It was like a scene from a very funny movie. Only it was real. And I was living it. See, it wasn't my awkwardness, or my looks, or my accent, or the color of my skin that stopped Joycell from wanting me. It was my religion. All those other attributes are malleable; you can break them down, remold them, and change them forever. Even skin color can be altered. But the one thing you cannot change is your past, your cultural background, where you come from. There we were, sweaty, yearning, fumbling, longing to connect, and the only thing that got in the way was the one thing I could not do anything about. But seriously, what had she been thinking this whole time? That I was a Jehovah's Witness?

After a silence as long as my penis, and almost as hard, I decided to leave. I thanked her for her hospitality and bent down to retrieve my DVD. I pressed eject and went to grab it, but the stupid-ass DVD would not come out. It was stuck. I kept tugging at it, trying to pry it from the death grip of the Mormon DVD player. But it wouldn't give. So I just left it there, half-stuck. I even left my CD in her stereo. It wasn't a graceful exit, but I was out of there nonetheless.

On the walk home I was hurting. I didn't understand what I had done wrong. I felt upset that I might have caused someone pain. I felt sheepish about my behavior with Joycell. I'd preyed on her loneliness, used it to my advantage. But the truth is, I was lonely, too. I was also away from family and friends and food I liked, and the warmth of my childhood bed. I was in a foreign country and I was trying so damn hard to fit in.

See, it was never really about getting a kiss; it was always about sharing a moment of intimacy with another person. To be touched and looked at and held like a living, breathing human being. We all want that. We all need that.

I often wonder what became of Joycell; I wonder if she's happily married to a nice Jewish guy and living in Brooklyn. I wonder if she ever thinks of that Thanksgiving we spent together. Most of all, I wonder if when she reads this she's going to sue me. And what became of my DVD? Crumpled and destroyed, probably. Fragments of it disintegrated into the earth. Forever sealed in the soil with a forbidden kiss on its lips. I imagine my CD still spinning, "Unchained Melody" forever stuck on repeat.

Chaos Theory

GROWING UP IN NEW DELHI WAS NOISY AND CHAOTIC. THIS is part of India's charm. Driving through New Delhi is like driving in a video game, because you're not only weaving through cars but also bicycles, cows, beggars, rickshaws, horses, and an occasional elephant. I love it. *Honk honk honk!* Everyone smashes on their horns nonstop, which creates something of a melody. The toot of a horn, much like the head bobble, can mean so many different things. We've created an entire language with how we toot our horn. You honk when you're overtaking someone, you honk when you're ten cars deep at a red light, you honk when you're feeling lonely. In India if you don't hear a horn, the only explanation is that the entire city has been blown up by a nuclear bomb. Or that you've lost your hearing.

There is constant noise in Delhi. At 5:30 a.m. the praying in the mosques starts, and they play this over loudspeakers so you can hear it in every corner of every neighborhood. The guy who collects the garbage comes by on a rickshaw, yelling. The guy who delivers the bread is shouting at us to come outside and pick it up. And since every house is stacked on top of each other, sometimes literally, we hear every neighbor's argument.

But you know what? I love the music of this noise. Back in LA, life is too quiet for me, even though people in smaller American towns think it's crazy to call LA "quiet." It is, though. And I miss the noise.

Judgment Day in Boise

"I'VE WANTED TO BE AN ACTOR SINCE I WAS A LITTLE BOY." That's what some people say. Or maybe, "I've always had a *calling*." Or better yet, "I feel it in my fingers, I feel it in my toes." Not me. No calling, no lifelong dream, no feeling in my toes, no inkling whatsoever that this was what I wanted to do. I had enrolled in the University of Portland's business program, focusing on marketing, because I was always fascinated with commercials, and thought maybe someday I'd make them. I wanted to be like those cool marketing executives at Nike who have handlebar mustaches and exhale smoke from the sides of their mouths.

Toward the end of my freshman year, on an evening stroll around the campus I decided to explore the theater building. In the lobby I saw all the head shots of the actors who were starring in the current play. *So many pretty girls*. Underneath the pictures a particular sign grabbed my attention. It read: "Auditions for *Ring Around the Moon*, Saturday, 3 p.m. to 6 p.m." I looked at the sign. I looked at the head shots. I looked back at the sign. I thought to myself, *Wait a minute; if I want to meet these pretty girls with the pretty head shots, then I should audition for this play! And they will all inevitably become my friends and subsequently my girlfriends!*

I went to the audition without a clue about what I was getting into. A crowd of theater students—older, cooler, theater-ier— huddled together in what, even then, I recognized as a clique.

"Hop up on the stage!" cried the head of the theater department, Dr. Ed Bowen, who also happened to be directing this play. (And no, he wasn't that kind of doctor, and yes he did have a PhD. And yes, you can get a doctorate in theater.)

"Hop up onstage!" he bellowed again.

I climbed up with the rest of the students.

"You're in the jungle! You're a monkey! Act like a monkey!"

So I flailed my arms and acted like a monkey.

"Now you're a dog!"

"You're a snake!"

After watching our movements for a few minutes, he sat us down on the stage and gave us the spiel about the play, explaining the parts that we could audition for. *Ring Around the Moon* is a 1950s British comedy of errors by Christopher Fry. I decided I would audition for the part of the elderly British butler. I was born in England and I could pull off a British accent pretty decently. (I don't *have* a British accent. I can just *do* one. All Indians can; we are taught the "Queen's English" in school.) And as for being an old man? No problemo. For my old-man audition I basically crouched down low and hunched my shoulders, fake limping with an imaginary cane. I looked like a 117-year-old grandpa who had Parkinson's on top of his leprosy. It was not my most finely honed or nuanced portrayal. Especially since the character, as written, was only in his sixties, with just a bit of stiffness to his walk. I played him like British Yoda.

I must have done something right, though, because the next

day I showed up at the theater to look at the casting list, and lo and behold, there was my name. Must have been the accent.

When I saw my name right there on the list next to the character of Joshua the Butler, I got incredibly excited. Not because I thought I had "found my calling" or anything, but because this meant, basically, that the other students would be forced to interact with me, and I would have more than one friend! They had no choice! I daydreamed about spending rehearsals and evenings with these artsy, exotic, theatrical people talking about music and poetry and right-brain things like that.

It's funny: if you look at the stereotypical hierarchy of high school and college social groups, theater kids are almost always viewed as the "weirdos" or maybe the "alternative kids"; they're certainly not viewed as being as weird as, say, the debate team or chess club kids, but they're still not really considered *cool*. But to me? This was Mecca. They were so confident and funny and different, and they dressed in things like Converse sneakers, torn jeans, and thick black-rimmed glasses before glasses were a thing. They all smoked cigarettes and had this blasé attitude about the world. These *were* the cool kids, in my book, and I wanted to join their gang.

❖

Let me just be honest and say that when it came to my acting, no one was calling me "the natural." I was pretty terrible. But at the time I didn't know it. There was a comfort, almost, in my ignorance of how badly I overacted. During rehearsals I remember thinking, *Oh my God, everyone here is such a good actor,* and the only way I knew to match their intensity was to BE LOUDER. They must have all wondered, *Why is Kunal always shouting?*

The more "famous" actors in the school (mind you, the entire theater program consisted of only forty kids) got all the lead parts and would walk away with all the glory. During rehearsals I would watch these other actors from afar. I made friends with a few of the lost souls like me. But what I really wanted was to be accepted by the guy and the girl playing the leads. I wanted so badly to be liked by them. I would stand in earshot of the famous ones and try to join the conversation every time they said something I understood. The truth is I wasn't great at understanding sarcasm, which seemed to be the root of all their jokes, so I just ended up laughing constantly at things I had no idea about. And because I was not standing directly in front of them or in the circle of people surrounding them, I now realize I just looked like a guy who enjoyed laughing at walls.

One day I asked one of these famous actors for some acting advice. "Is it funnier if I say this line in a high pitch like a girl? Or a low baritone pitch like a macho dude?"

The two of us were standing apart from the group, in private.

"Kunal," he said, louder than he needed to, "it's not *how* you say it; it's about the motivation of what you're saying. *Ugh*." He spoke so loud that the other actors turned around to listen. "It's not about saying the line *high*, or saying the line *low*. It's about what you really mean in this moment. Stop trying so hard to sell the joke." He stormed off with an air of indignation.

I felt naked and on display. It seemed like the entire room was judging me, mocking me, and making *me* the butt of their sarcastic jokes. What he said made sense, actually, and it wasn't bad advice, but ironically it wasn't *what* he said; it's *how* he said it. He could have said, *Hey, Kunal, I know you're trying really hard, but here's something you could think about.*

You know that feeling when you really look up to someone, and you muster up the courage to ask them what, in your mind, is a great question, and you play that moment in your head over and over again, and you fantasize about how that person is going to think you're so smart for asking this great question, and how you're going to become best buds, but instead they make you seem dumb and small and unworthy? Like asking for an autograph from your favorite celebrity and they not only roll their eyes and keep walking, but they also go on live television and call you a mumbling, bumbling idiot of a fool? This was that moment. I felt like a mumbling, bumbling idiot of a fool.

That moment shook my confidence. Suddenly I became worried about whether I was overacting. *Is this subtle enough? Do I mean it?* Up until that point, when I was rehearsing for *Ring Around the Moon*, Professor Ed never told me to do *less*. He always told me to do more. He always told me to go for it. And he loved it! I had so much confidence because he allowed me to be funny. This was better for my evolution as an actor and he knew it; there's a reason he was chair of the department, and not Mr. Wannabe Famous Actor.

When I look back at that scolding, I will never forget how small it made me feel, and I'm reminded of a very important lesson that I learned that day. If I were ever fortunate to be in a position where someone needed my advice, I would never make him or her feel stupid or small. I would always give them my time.

❖

The night of the first dress rehearsal had arrived and there was chaos in my brain. Because in the dressing room EVERYONE WAS WALKING AROUND NAKED. As if boobies and peens didn't matter. Just like that. Girls and guys running around, bouncy boobs, floppy peens, helping each other into costumes. Obviously, I began to have an anxiety attack; I didn't want to take off my clothes in front of all these people. It was hard enough trying to be accepted; now I had to show them all my hooded peen?

"Hurry up! Put it on! Here, I'll help." One of the costume girls ran over with my butler costume and began helping me out of my clothes.

I was so nervous. My hands were shaking as I took off my clothes; I was wearing these stupid gray leopard undies that had a little tear on the right butt cheek. They were my brother's. I hated that I was wearing those; I hated that I had even accepted them when Mom handed them down to me. I changed very quickly. The costume girl could tell I was nervous, and she thought it was because this was my first play. I gladly used that excuse as she helped me into the suit. I thanked her. I let out a deep sigh. "Cute undies, by the way," she murmured as she walked away.

Then, as if my heart weren't already about to burst, the head of the costume department came around the corner and told me that I had to lather white shoe polish all over my hair.

"Shoe polish in my hair?" I asked, as we all do—repeat a statement as a question when we think it's absurd.

"Yes," she said. "To age you. You look too young."

Of course I look too young, shithead. I'm eighteen and my character is sixty-something.

She tossed me the tube. "Oh, and take off your suit, because you don't want any of that stuff on the costume."

"You want me to take off my suit?" I asked.

"Yes, always put on makeup before you get into costume."

Stupid shit, dude. That meant that I had to undress, sit there in my gray torn underwear, and apply white shoe polish to my hair.

Then it was showtime. "Five minutes to curtain!" the stage manager yelled. I began pacing back and forth, reciting my lines over and over in my head. My scalp was getting sweaty and white shoe polish began to seep into my eyes. "Are you crying?" a cast-mate asked. "Yes," I lied. "I'm just emotional right now," I said, hiding the fact that a hole was burning through my iris. "Places!" the stage manager bellowed as we huddled behind the curtain, nervously anticipating for it to rise. I heard a large mechanical noise and the curtains began to lift. At first the stage lights, designed to illuminate the actors' faces, were blinding. It took me a few seconds to focus on the seated audience. The two leads of the play began the scene effortlessly as I (the butler) puttered around in the background fixing drinks. With every laugh I could feel the energy of the audience on my skin. When it was my time to speak, I was surprised at how naturally all of the instincts came to me. All the time put in rehearsal seemed to have paid off, as I, too, began to fall into a very cathartic rhythm. In the second act, my character was supposed to come onto the stage and catch his boss snogging his mistress. The line on the page was "Oh," as in a very subtle exclamation of surprise from this very well-mannered butler. I, however, was overcome with the sudden desire to yell my line at the top of my lungs. As I let out a very loud "OH!" the audience erupted in laughter; this made my blood rush, as I, unscripted, let out another loud "Oh" and then another, and another, until the audience erupted in applause. I could see the lead actor did not enjoy this much, but I didn't give two shits, because something in me had changed. I had the whole audience on my side, and I was hooked on that feeling. After the play ended, high on having successfully finished my first performance, I was strutting around the dressing room when Dr. Ed Bowen poked his head in and asked to speak with me. I figured he was going to give me a pat on the back, but instead he said, "I know you trusted your instinct, and that was fine, but next time, can you tone it down a little, please?" This didn't hurt my feelings in any way. After all, he was the director and he had put it so gently that I understood not to take too much liberty with my lines. What did hurt me was applying white shoe polish to my hair every night over the entire run of the play and crying my way to the opening curtain.

In the end it was all worth it. I had made a few friends during the course of the play. Not friends that I considered close at the time, but people friendly enough that I could say hi to them when I ran into them during school hours. The play itself, *Ring Around the Moon*, apparently was a hit. We got good reviews. And despite the overacting of my geriatric 189-year-old butler, we were accepted into the regional finals of the American College Theater Festival (ACTF), which is essentially the World Cup of college theater. We took the play on the road and headed to the fabled place that every actor dreams about, that star-studded city where so many legendary careers have been launched: Boise, Idaho.

❖

I'd like to tell you about all the fond memories I have of exploring Idaho. Except that I have zero memories of exploring Idaho. We were stuck in the frickin' hotel for three days, and I stayed in my room and watched TV while the other actors partied together. It was my first trip outside of my college with people that I didn't know very well. Mostly it was my fault. I was insecure, and a lot of that was from thinking people did not like me because I was different. Which I later discovered was not true. I think it is common for people to do that, to live in a shell protecting themselves from an imaginary enemy.

Since the end of the play's run we had done a few extra rehearsals. I had worked out all the kinks in my performance, perfecting my old-man walk. I even played around with a few of my lines, trying to get them to sound more old, or to get more of a laugh out of people. We felt ready. *I* felt ready.

We finally performed the play for the judges at ACTF, and when it was over and we took our bows I felt so proud, so elated, like I had achieved something important. After the performance, once the applause faded and the crowd trickled out of the auditorium, we peeled off our costumes and then came back to the stage to receive our "notes" from the panel of "adjudicators."

I still had the white shoe polish in my hair. I could feel the sticky goo on my scalp; it was really beginning to harden under all my sweat. I stood with my castmates, shoulder to shoulder, waiting to hear how the judges would score us. I had only the vaguest sense that for the rest of the cast, this was the biggest deal of their lives. If we made it out of regionals then we would advance to the national finals in Washington, D.C., and the seniors and juniors would have a shot at booking a professional job or, better yet, an agent. This could slingshot them to glory. I was just a freshman who was there for shits and giggles, but for my older castmates, this marked the difference between an acting career and no acting career. This was the first time I realized that the stakes in this business can be so incredibly high. I mean, not "curing cancer" high, or "rescuing children from burning buildings" high, but if your play doesn't advance, or if your pilot isn't picked up, or if your movie doesn't get distribution, then suddenly you can't pay your mortgage, you can't afford your children's education, you can't keep your health care.

The doors to the auditorium opened. The judges entered. They were old and crusty, these gargoyle-looking men with thick beards and deep, gravelly voices. They looked like they'd just been pried from the stucco walls of the theater, where they'd been affixed for the past hundred years.

The first adjudicator cleared his throat. "I'd like to begin by discussing the play's realism." He looked down at his notes. "As an example, let's take the case of the butler. Played by . . . COOONEL?" He looked toward me. "It's like he's in an entirely different world. Let's just take one specific moment where COOONEL is surprised by something, and he makes an *Ooooohh* sound, and then he turns around and says the same thing to the other side of the stage. No one would ever do that."

The second judge spoke up. "I had an issue with the way people were talking to each other. Let's just take, as an example," he said, flipping through his notes, "KAANAL. I don't understand why he's talking louder than everyone else. It just takes me out of this world."

The third judge frowned, glancing down at his notes. "I, too, had a problem with the play's realism. Just as one example . . . COOONEL. I'm sorry to harp on you, but—"

And so it continued. The judges ripped the play and they shredded me to pieces. We filed out of the auditorium, and no one talked to me about the comments. No one accused me of botching the play, no one said they were upset with me, no one talked to me about my "realism." This is because no one talked to me, period. I was left alone. Everyone went out and partied and I returned to my hotel room.

Was I the reason we didn't advance to the finals? It's hard to say. Maybe my performance really was so awful that it handicapped our chances. Or maybe the judges hated pretty much everything about the play and I'm only remembering the notes directed at me.

Over the years I've thought about this a lot, and about how, as an actor, there are so many things out of your control. For example, let's just say you're an actor and you book your dream TV role. You're about to show up for your first day of production, and then the executive producer, after googling you, sees that you're thirty-two but they have cast you as a twenty-three-year-old. This puts a tiny poisonous thought in his head, and he makes a phone call to the studio head. The studio head says, "Who cares, he looks twenty-three and that's all that counts." And then the studio head tells his wife about it at dinner while eating sushi, and the wife says, well, maybe the audience will find out that he really is thirty-two and that could lead to teenage girls finding him too old. That tiny poisonous thought has now worked its way from executive producer to studio head to his wife's head and back into the studio head's head. And it is not such a tiny thought any longer. So when the studio head goes to sleep that night, he has a dream that the reviews for his new show—his baby—are mostly positive, except the reviews all said the same thing: the actor is thirty-two, and this led to the audience becoming so outraged that they staged a protest and marched upon the studio, leading to the studio head's downfall and eventual early demise.

So the next day . . . you're fired, even though you really were great in the part and do look twenty-three.

Things have to align themselves so perfectly in our universe for actors to make a paycheck. Maybe this was how my *Ring Around the Moon* castmates felt—that *I* was the wild card that cost them their ticket to the finals, that I was the one variable out of their control. I don't know.

What I do know is that once those notes finally sank in, once I internalized what had happened, I didn't feel bad for myself anymore. I didn't mope. I knew that a great deal of investment and sacrifice had gone into me coming to this country, and I simply just didn't have the luxury or the time to feel sorry for myself.

I accepted I was not a good actor.

And I resolved one thing: *I need to get better.*

A Thought Recorded on an Aeroplane Cocktail Napkin

There is a lot in this world to be worried about . . . but there is also a lot to celebrate. Don't be a worrier. Be a smiler. Be a boss.

The Girl I Went to Mass For

ALLISON WAS STRONGER THAN ME. A REALLY STRONG GIRL. Muscular. A jaw like a linebacker. She had calluses on her hands and feet. She played soccer. She wore a cross. She always smiled. And she had eyes that were a shade I had never seen in my life. Gray. Gray eyes. I loved those eyes. I loved those calluses and those triceps. She was nice to me, too. We would take walks on campus in the evening. Sometimes she would wrap my arms in hers. I would later go home alone and . . . you know . . . I was alone. I asked her to be my date to the college dance. It was on a boat. Why are all college socials on boats? I wonder what they do when schools aren't near a lake or the coast. Hmmm. I borrowed a black jacket from my brother. It was a nice black jacket, way too big for me. He is a few inches taller with broad shoulders, so all his hand-me-downs were like wearing a blanket.

On the bus to the college dance, Allison and I were sitting together. She was always a close talker. Always. I never minded. Her breath always smelled like mint. We were close talking, and I was telling her about India, and she was so interested in it all. Not "Do you have camels?" interested, more like, "Wow, how many cousins do you have again?" The more we talked the closer her face got to mine. She asked for a mint. I thought I had some in my left pocket, but I didn't. What I did have in my left pocket was something that my brother had left there "by mistake."

"What's this?" I said, holding it up. A condom. A ninety-nine-cent condom. She was aghast. My mind racing, I searched for the right thing to say, but I think what came out was one big "Uhhh-hhh."

"What kind of girl do you think I am, Kunal?" (You know you're in trouble when they use your name.)

"Um, it's my brother's jacket. I had no idea. I'm so sorry."

"We're not even dating! How could you think of me like that?" And then she said those dreaded words, "You're like a *brother* to me."

A brother? A brother? Was she about to tie a Rakhi band on my wrist? What about the close talking? And the loving-India thing? And the asking for a mint? Of course I said none of this. I just apologized. Truth is, it wasn't my condom. I didn't actually think I was going to get laid. I just wanted someone to treat me like I wasn't this weird skinny Indian guy aimlessly navigating his way through social etiquette. Someone to treat me *like a person*. I had found that person. And her name was Allison. But I pulled out a condom and showed it to her. She went and sat in an empty seat on the bus. I was surprised how upset she was. I mean, seriously, what's the big deal? So I thought you were beautiful and loved you and wanted to make sweet love to you (apparently). Why create such a fuss? Just accept the apology and move on.

I sat on the bus contemplating whether to go on the boat with the rest of the group. I tried making an excuse about getting seasick. But the bus driver wouldn't allow me to sit on the bus during the dance. Some policy about safety, he said. Plus all the guys and their dates were looking at me weirdly. So I just got on that stupid boat, and I went to that dance alone.

❖

"Would you be willing to go to Mass with me?" Allison asked me a few weeks later. She said that she had prayed about it and that she was willing to forgive me. I thanked her and apologized again. Yes. Of course I would go to Mass with her. I would have climbed Everest naked for her.

We went to Mass. It was lovely. I find pretty much all religion lovely. After the service, everyone was asked to speak about something positive in their lives. I spoke about this "angel" in my life. About how she had saved me. I made most of it up on the spot but it felt true in the moment. I was on a spiritual high, plus I really wanted her to like me again—friend, brother, lover, whatever she wanted, I just wanted her back. It was a nice way to encapsulate my long-winded apology. After Mass ended, we were allowed to hug everyone. I specifically stole some hugs from a few people so it would work out that we hugged last. And then we did. We hugged, and for me it was the hug of a lifetime. Then, involuntarily, I whispered breathily in her ear, "Finally." I meant it. It was creepy, but I meant it.

Allison transferred colleges a year later. Next time she came to town, she seemed different. Everything was different. I was more acclimated to the United States, more confident, more myself. I took her out for a couple of drinks to catch up. A few drinks turned into more, and some more after that. We ended up making out.

It was awful. The entire fantasy I'd imagined for so long was replaced with what seemed like two high school students fumbling in the dark. Something just didn't feel right. We stopped. I looked away, embarrassed. Confused. *Was it me?* As she gathered her things to leave, she said she was sorry. "Because," she said, "truth is, Kunal, I'm a lesbian."

Apparently throughout the two years we were friends, she was fighting through the confusion, the pain, the . . . whatever you go through when you realize that what your body is telling you is against everything you've ever been taught as a child. I thanked her for her honesty. I told her she could call me anytime she needed someone to talk to. This angel. This prophecy. This goddess on a pedestal. She seemed to be exhausted from wrestling with this perceived "sinful sexual orientation," her religion versus her desire, and I felt bad for her.

After she left, I went to eat a bacon cheeseburger. It was a really good burger and it made me think about my own religious beliefs. About religion versus desire. Was it right to eat beef when doing so was so completely against everything I was taught as a child? Did that make me a sinner? And if so, should I too be as morally conflicted as Allison? And then it hit me. I just really liked beef. Allison just really liked women. And if God really gave a damn he would have struck us both down with lightning for our sins. You see, in my opinion, God didn't care if I ate beef, or if Allison ate . . . was a lesbian. He only cared that I tipped the waiter who brought me my burger and that Allison lived a life that made her happy and let her find love. To this day every time I eat a bacon cheeseburger, I think about Allison the Lesbian.

❖

I'm a horrible manager of pee. I always hold
it till the last moment. I'm not sure why. I'm
not someone who is usually a procrastinator.
But something about peeing . . .

Kumar Ran a Car

THE SUMMER BEFORE MY SENIOR YEAR I DECIDED THAT I WAS done working outdoors or collecting garbage. I wanted something indoors, preferably work you did while sitting on a chair, in a room with an air conditioner. I flipped through the student paper and saw an opening in the computer lab. *Perfect.* Except for the fact that I knew nothing about computers, everything about this job was appealing. I mean, I could turn one on, but I didn't know how to code. Or how to program. Or how to troubleshoot. All I knew was that if something goes wrong, you should probably unplug the computer for thirty seconds. But I thought, *Hey, I'm Indian, maybe I can just say that and they'll trust that I know what I'm doing.*

I interviewed with this quiet guy who wore glasses, named Dominick. He was from China. His hair was perfectly parted to one side, polo buttoned all the way to the top, and he wore light brown khakis and Nike running sneakers.

"Hi, Kunal, nice to meet you," he said, in a soft, high-pitched voice that sounded like an adorable old lady. I could tell right away that the poor guy must have had a rough childhood.

"I am looking for some people to be computer lab managers. What are your skills?"

"Troubleshooting, programming, Excel, PowerPoint," I said, dropping in every piece of jargon I could think of.

"Mac or PC?"

"I can do Mac, I can do PC, I can do all Cs," I said, laughing.

"Can you give me more specifics?"

"You know how it is. I grew up in India. I've been taking apart computers my whole life. I know how the computer *thinks*. I know how it moves. I'm always one step ahead of it."

He nodded. The Indian thing really impressed him. "I like you. I'm going to hire you."

We shook hands. Bingo!

"Given your advanced skill set, I'm going to give you a very special project." He turned to the computer and opened up a software program I had never seen. "The school is trying to integrate this new voice recognition software. I want you to figure it out, dissect it, and write an entire instruction manual based on what you've learned."

"Cool, I'm on it." *Kill me now.*

So three days a week, four hours each shift, my job was to sit at the computer and become an expert in this software. Given my advanced-skills status, Dominick gave me my own computer lab—just one room with one computer—so that I wouldn't be disturbed from my task. My job was to write a thirty-page manual for software that made utterly no sense to me.

The program, essentially, was an early-early-early version of Siri. Except that it didn't really work and it had all these complicated menus and options that I found insanely baffling. The first day I took the job very seriously. I spoke into the microphone and compared what I said to the words that appeared on the screen:

"The cat drank the cow's milk," I said.

On-screen: *Kangaroos in Australia are part of the binary world.*

It probably didn't help that I had an Indian accent.

I just sat there for hours, carefully repeating sentence after sentence, watching as the monitor butchered every word. I would click menu options and the cursor would just keep blinking, confused. Maybe Raj could have solved this puzzle if he'd existed then, but it was too much for Kunal.

I spent an entire day just getting the program to say my name correctly.

"Kunal Nayyar."

Kumar. Ran. A. Car.

Whatevs. I basically gave up on the project after a few days, and each shift I would spend fifteen minutes on voice recognition, then the rest of the afternoon in Yahoo! chat rooms. Those were big in 2000. I loved that you could explore all these subcultures and just start chatting with people anonymously. My screen name was "Tan_Skinned_Man." I chatted with women all over the world and told them I was a professional tennis player.

"Kunal?" Dominick asked from outside the door. I always kept the door locked.

"One minute," I said, alt-tabbing from the chat rooms and opening the software.

"Why do you lock the door?"

"You know me. I can only focus when no one's disturbing me."

He clapped me on the shoulder. "I understand. Keep up the good work."

I felt a little bad for deceiving Dominick, and I also felt bad that he was the butt of many of my jokes. I'm sorry to say, I made fun of his voice a lot. He also had something of a reputation as a mean boss, and I wasn't the only one doing imitations of him behind his back.

A week before the project was due, I still had absolutely nothing to show for it. Just a blank Word document. "Do you mind showing me your progress?" Dominick asked.

"It's not perfect yet. And I only deliver perfect."

"No problem. I understand," he said, leaving me alone with the cyber-tennis-chicks.

I realized I would soon be fired. So I decided, *Screw it, I'm just going to write something.*

So I just started making stuff up.

"Once you press File, the Command Screen will open up."

"Use the right mouse button to initiate a conversation."

"Click the L button three times to indicate that you LOVE this software." It was practically that bad.

The week passed and it was time to face the music. I would tell Dominick that I'd been struggling, that I'd given it my damnedest, but it might be too faulty a system to properly document. Tail between my legs, I entered his office.

"Kunal. I'm glad you came," he said, shooting me a hard look.

Shit. Did he find out about the Yahoo! chats?

"I just got an email from the university. I have some troubling news."

Shit. My scholarships.

Dominick took off his glasses. "The school has decided to recall the software. It's not working properly. There are some disagreements with the licensor. So there will be no need for the manual."

"That's terrible."

"Kunal, I'm so sorry. I know how hard you've been working."

"It's okay," I said. "Whatever's best for the university."

"Should we take a look at what you've written so far?"

"Honestly, Dominick, given this development, I'm not sure I feel comfortable with that. Maybe it's best for me to shred all the documentation so there's not a paper trail? What if someone sues or something?"

"Good point, good point. Do that," he said. "Because of your hard work and commitment to this project, I'm going to promote you to lab manager of the engineering building."

He gave me a raise, bumping me up to nine dollars an hour, which was damn good money at the time. I would manage the school's flagship computer lab, the one that had just received the brand-new translucent Macs.

And as for the fact that I'm computer illiterate? Well . . . "Your only job is to maintain the lab, make sure it's clean, manage the technicians," said Dominick. "If anyone has a real problem with the new Macs, there will be a specialist."

"Yeah, those new Macs, I've read up on them, they're a strange beast," I said.

"Exactly. Not even *I* know the ins and outs."

Amazingly, it turns out I was a pretty competent lab manager. I was good with people, treated the employees with respect, and most important, was excellent at getting someone else to solve the real problems. My lab even got voted the most user-friendly lab in the university.

Maybe Dominick thought of me as a protégé of sorts. One night as I sat on the stoop of my house strumming my guitar, I saw Dominick crossing the street in front of me. He wore a red polo shirt buttoned to the top, and it was a little weird seeing him outside the lab.

"Hey, Dominick," I called.

He hesitated for a second, and then came and joined me on the stoop. "Play me a song, Kunal."

I could tell something was bothering him. He looked melancholy.

So I played him a melancholy tune. After I was done, he said, "Beautiful. Play it one more time, please." So I did. As I was playing, Dominick began to tear up. After I finished, he told me about how he missed his home in China, that he wished he could see his family, and that he often felt very alone.

"Many people think I'm an angry guy," he said. "That I fire people because I'm cruel. But the truth is that I *have* to run a tight ship, because my education is on the line. If I don't have this job then I can't pay for my studies."

He wiped the tears from his cheeks. And I felt guilty, because I too had made jokes and laughed at his expense. *Ha ha, Dominick with the high voice and the face that looks like an owl.*

"It's going to be okay, Dominick," I said, awkwardly patting him on the back.

"Thanks," he said, suddenly embarrassed. He had opened the door and I just didn't deliver my support.

"I'll see you around," he said sheepishly as he walked away.

"Righto," was all I could manage.

After he left, I found myself feeling empty. I was disappointed in myself for not lending him more of a shoulder to cry on. I could have said that I understood what it was like to assimilate. Or that I too knew what it felt like to be away from home. I mean, it wasn't that long ago that I myself had worn the ill-fitting shirts and corduroy pants, and people made fun of me behind my back. I could have said all of this. I could have been his good friend. Instead, I just said, "Righto." And to be honest, I have no idea why.

Sometimes we have "time machine moments" where we wish we could go back in time and fix our biggest mistakes. But sometimes we wish we could go back in time and fix the tiny ones, too.

❖

It drives me nuts when Microsoft Word shows me a green squiggly line under something I've written. It makes me want to reach through the computer screen and choke the life out of Microsoft Word. As if it were a person standing in my front yard challenging my ability to protect my family. Green squiggly. Huh, I know better than you, stupid machine corrector. I hate you. My sentences are perfection constructed, purely.

Lollipops and Crisps

GRACE. A PHENOMENAL ACTRESS, TRULY GIFTED, THE BELLE of every ball. Big eyes, milky skin, and short-cropped black hair. She was the Audrey Hepburn of the theater department. I wanted to *be* her. She was, of course, hundreds and thousands of miles out of my league. She was so divine that I didn't even *consider* her as a possible love interest. She was just a fantasy, a whispering dream. Also, she was a senior and I was a junior, and I didn't exactly have the strongest track record with older women. (Exhibits A, B, and C: Ishani.) In three years Grace and I had maybe exchanged eleven words. I basically had Raj's selective mutism.

It started on what I will call "Eyeball Night." We had just thrown a wrap party for our production of *The Rose Tattoo*, and this night, like every night in Portland, was chilly and rainy. I sat in the backyard next to the keg, on the stoop, tugging my hoodie so close to my body that I looked like an egg.

Grace sat down next to me.

She's sitting next to me.

"Kooooooonel," she said, intentionally mispronouncing my name in a deep, cartoonish voice, almost like a female Colonel Sanders.

HOLY SHIT SHE'S TALKING TO ME. IS THIS REAL LIFE?

She was wearing a yellow rain jacket, white jeans, and a perfume called Egyptian Musk. (Even now that smell drives me crazy; one of the costume girls on *The Big Bang Theory* wears it, and it's a problem.) I couldn't think of anything to say.

Talk about anything, Kunal! You're from India, that's exotic, use it!

Mercifully it began to drizzle. . . .

"Wanna go inside?" I said.

"Sure."

We joined the larger crowd inside and she peeled off her jacket. She was wearing a button-down flowery shirt, and since the top three buttons were undone I was treated to a hint of cleavage; even better, as every guy knows, when a woman wears an oversize shirt with a wide collar, if she leans too far to the left or too far to the right, you can catch a glimpse of her body that you are not supposed to glimpse. I definitely glimpsed.

Grace grabbed a seat on the back of the couch—not sitting on the couch proper, and not sitting on the armrest, but actually perching high on the back of the couch, leaning her shoulders against the wall. I thought that was so goddamn cool that I stole the move from her—I still sit like that on couches. There were a bunch of drunk theater kids and the conversation turned sexual, which it often did at our parties. Someone asked loudly, "What's the most public place you've ever had sex?"

"What's your most sensitive spot?" someone else asked.

"Where's the weirdest place someone's ever licked you?" another asked.

Grace suddenly piped up. "Someone asked to lick my eyeball."

"Eyeball?" I said as everyone laughed.

"Kooooooonel," she said. "Do you want to lick my eyeball?"

"Lick your eyeball?" I asked, buying some time before I had to answer.

"Do you want to lick my eyeball?" she repeated.

"Okay, yeah, sure, I'll lick your eyeball."

"You don't sound so sure, Kooooooonel."

I took a breath.

"Grace. I will lick your eyeball."

Are people watching? Grace enjoyed a lofty position on the social ladder in the theater hierarchy; all eyes were on her constantly. I was suddenly self-conscious.

"Do it, Koooooonel." She opened her eyes wide and lifted her left eyelid with her fingers, the way you do when you're popping in your contacts.

She had such big, beautiful hazel-brown eyes. Eyes that always had the glimmer of hope. Eyes that said to anyone she focused her gaze on, *You are the only thing that matters to me in this room.*

I stared at that lovely dark left eye and realized that I couldn't bring myself to do it.

"Stop being such a pussy!" she said in a gravelly voice.

"It's just, I mean, I have a very short, stubby tongue; it might hurt."

"Very well then. Be a girl. Would you let me lick your eyeball?"

"I really wish I could remove the word *eye* from your question," I quipped, surprising myself with the bold and clever retort.*

The crowd around us seemed to fade away into darkness. They were anonymous extras in our big scene—we were in a slow-

---

* In hindsight, I think I may have thought of that line later, but for the sake of this particular story, let's just say I came up with it right then and there.

motion movie bubble; this was my *Notting Hill* moment; she was Julia Roberts and I was Hugh Grant. I opened my left eye as wide as I could. Huh, funny, we both picked left. She leaned in close as I caught a whiff of that soft Egyptian Musk and extended her adorable little tongue and touched the tip of my eyeball. This was our first kiss.

My eye involuntarily closed, and she pulled back. I could tell she was a little shy, almost as if we had just made out in church. "I'm going to get some wine," she said as she hopped off the couch.

"I'm going to rinse out my eye."

*Good one, Kunal.**

As the party began to dissolve I had a quick meeting with myself. *Okay, buddy, you've just been licked in the eye by the most beautiful girl in all the world; don't push your luck tonight; go home to bed and leave her wanting more.* So I decided to say my good-byes to everyone, hoping that I would have one more interaction with Grace before I left. I saw her standing next to a box of wine. Boxed wine, creating hangovers since 1967. I leaned in for a hug and said, "It was fun hanging out with you tonight."

"Same."

I loved the way she said that. Not "I feel the same" or even "The same." *Same.*

We parted ways and I went home to bed.

Then, at 4 a.m., I heard a knock on the window.

"Kooooooooooonel."

Transfixed in wonder, I let her in without saying a word.

She climbed into bed with me.

---

* That one I *did* say.

❖

The next morning I woke up wondering if it was all a dream. *She was still right there.* I studied her face as she slept. Painting her portrait in my mind. She was breathtakingly beautiful, at peace it seemed; a steady rhythm to her breathing; gently smiling. *She. Was. Perfect.*

"I was a little *drunkst* last night," she said when she woke.

Drunkst. Adorable. I was so hooked already. She liked to make up words. And she did this thing where she'd look down when she was thinking about what to say, and then, just before she was about to make a point, she'd look up at you, like in the movies. Truth is that I fell in love with her the second she asked me to lick her eyeball. I loved her even before I knew her. And since *everyone else* was in love with her, too, I couldn't believe my luck that she had somehow picked *me*. After she left my house, I did a twenty-minute happy dance in front of the mirror. I hopped into the shower with a spring in my step. Later that day I saw Grace again, in the lobby of the theater. We hugged this time, holding on just a second longer than necessary, and I felt her squeeze my back firm enough to signal that something had happened; that something was real.

We soon began to see more of each other; we even began holding hands in public. Without ever having "the Talk" we were becoming a couple. Grace taught me a lot of things about a lot of things. But she *really* taught me how to listen to music. Before Grace, for example, I never really thought that deeply about music. I mean I loved music, and I loved playing guitar and singing and such, but I never really had the bandwidth to comprehend how much good music there is in the world. I mainly listened to radio-friendly bands like Dave Matthews and Creed and Jason Mraz, but she introduced me to a darker world of Radiohead and Björk.

"Listen to the lyrics, Kunal," she always said. "Listen to what they're saying."

As bubbly as she was, Grace always had an innate darkness to her. It may have been an actor thing. We're all masochistic.

"Listen to this song," she said one day and played me Radiohead's "True Love Waits." It didn't do much for me.

I suppose it was a new sound to me. I was mostly used to hearing songs in major keys. This was different. I didn't get it.

"*Listen*," she said again. I listened a second time and I still struggled to feel whatever it was that she was trying to make me feel. She played it a third time and a fourth. Still nothing. Then she told me how the song had come to be made. I learned that Thom Yorke, who wrote the song, had read in the newspaper about a missing child who was trapped in a London cellar. The child survived for three days on only lollipops and crisps (potato chips). The song is about this missing child yearning to live, hence the lyric: "True love waits on lollipops and crisps."

"Play it one more time," I said.

And then I heard it.

"True love waits. True love waits. On lollipops and crisps."

The song sprang to life in my heart. All the minor notes and the odd key shifts that didn't make sense began to flow through me like lava. It wasn't about the catchy chorus or the sing-a-long lyrics I was used to; it was about something real, and the connection I felt to that song in that moment was not something I had felt before.

❖

I was intoxicated. I had fallen in love with Grace. I liked it.

She also taught me about things like vintage stores, ironic T-shirts, Converse sneakers, record stores, and the farmers' market. Soon I even started dressing like her, wearing red sneakers, bootleg jeans, and torn and scrubby ironic T-shirts. My favorite T-shirt to this day is a dirty white one that says "Brown" on it. She taught me how to make hummus and cucumber sandwiches on pita bread. Which is made exactly the way it sounds.* She taught me how to explore my dark side. I've always been the kind of person who wakes up happy. If I'm having a bad day I can shake it off with a smile. But Grace encouraged me to explore something deeper. She asked me all sorts of questions about how I was feeling, and why. I was used to masking my pain through humor and she wanted me to wear my pain on my sleeve. She said, "It's okay to feel." "You don't have to pretend." "Enjoy the melancholy."

Before I knew it I was drinking black coffee, smoking cigarettes, wearing torn jeans and vintage T-shirts, and listening to Radiohead on repeat. I was so emo and I was loving it. Because for the first time in America, I felt like I had an identity.

❖

She taught me how to make love.

❖

Many months flew by like this—hanging out in the park, listening to gut-wrenching music, laughing, watching old sketch comedy shows like *The State* and classic *SNL*. She loved making me peanut

---

* I like it when the name of a food is also the recipe for making it.

butter and jelly sandwiches with the crusts cut off. Grace was my first real-life girlfriend. And I was eating it up.

I never thought about the fact that she would graduate in May. Or that she would ever graduate. Or that we would have to talk someday about our relationship, or anything that could ever take me away from my first true love.

Grace got cast in a play that I was not in. I was busy prepping for another play that semester. This meant that since she was in rehearsals all evening, I wouldn't have a chance to see her until 10:00 p.m. This began to gnaw at me. And all these thoughts began to creep into my brain. I envisioned her shooting the shit with her castmates, chatting and gossiping with them, maybe talking about our relationship. Maybe flirting with the other actors.

I began to see less and less of her. This led to a vicious cycle: the less I saw of her, the more I *wanted* to see her. I remember calling her cell phone as soon as the rehearsals ended at ten o'clock, and sometimes she would call me right back but sometimes she wouldn't. Sometimes I wouldn't get a call back until ten thirty. Sometimes eleven. Sometimes not at all.

One night I called her at 10:10 (I knew she'd be home), no answer, then 10:17, no answer, then at 10:45 she picked up the phone.

"I just got home," she said.

"Don't rehearsals end at ten?" I could hear the desperation in my voice.

"Dude," she said. "Dude, just relax, okay?"

Dude. *Dude?*

We eventually did hang out that night. All would be well. It's interesting how we can go from severe insecurity about a relationship to absolute security as soon you see that person face-to-face. We make monsters in our head when we're alone, and they just as quickly vanish when you're together. All I wanted was to see her, to make her happy. But part of me was beginning to turn resentful. I wanted her to *know* that I was trying to make her happy, and I wanted *her* to know that *I* knew that *she* wasn't working as hard for *my* happiness. For example, I knew that she wanted to go to the Rufus Wainwright concert. The tickets were expensive but I wanted her to be happy, so for her birthday I bought her one ticket. *One* ticket.

My gift was laced with acid. I wanted her to see that they were expensive and that she should feel guilty that she could go and I could not. I wanted to kill her with kindness so she could never leave me.

"Dude, this is silly, you have to come with me!" she said.

I let her ask me three or four times before I acquiesced and bought a ticket for myself. At the concert I sang loudly to "Cigarettes and Chocolate Milk."

"Shhhhhhhhhhh," she said. "Don't sing, just listen." That hurt my feelings. Everything was hurting my feelings. You see, it wasn't about her anymore; it was beginning to become about me.

One night I arrived late to a party and saw her leaning against a tree, smoking, talking to a guy covered in tattoos. He was strong looking, ripped in ways that I was not. He was wearing a whole string of earrings. He looked so damn cool, and I could tell from his body language that he liked her. Worse, I had a feeling that she liked him, too.

"I'm Jeff," he said, shaking my hand.

"Strong grip," I said, wishing I had met his hand with the same force.

"Hi, baby," I said to Grace.

She side-hugged me and kissed me on the cheek. Not on the lips.

On the cheek. Was she distant? I couldn't tell anymore. The three of us made some dumb, uneasy small talk and I learned that Jeff loved surfing and dogs, and that he drove a green Volkswagen bus.

"I'm not feeling that great," I said, hoping Grace would take her eyes off this guy and go home with me.

"Oh, do you mind if I stay?" she asked.

"Of course not," I lied.

I hugged her good-bye and we didn't kiss, again. I had a bad feeling in the pit of my stomach. It was the kind of feeling that just grows, and it grows and grows and grows and you can't do anything about it.

The next morning I had to drive to the grocery store to pick up some batteries, and by coincidence (not by coincidence) I passed Grace's house. I looked at her place like I always did. And parked next to her door was a green Volkswagen bus.

❖

I took a breath and decided to call her from the car, just to see how she would react.

"Hey, I'm at the store; want something?" I asked.

Silence.

"No, I'm good," she finally said. "See you later?"

I drove home, shaking with anger, sadness, confusion. All the monsters in my head were coming true.

I didn't call her all day. Around 10:20 p.m. my phone rang.

"Come over tonight," she said.

"I saw his bus."

She didn't say anything. Her silence made her sound like she was staring at the floor.

"Did you hook up?"

She began to cry and said, "I don't want to break up with you, Kunal, but what's the point? I'm graduating soon. In May I'm gone. So what are we doing anyway?" Her response was brilliant. She had accomplished several things:

1. She didn't confess to hooking up with him.

2. But she didn't deny it.

3. She didn't break up with me.

4. But she implied that we should be broken up.

We had reached an unspoken stalemate. We were still boyfriend and girlfriend without being boyfriend and girlfriend.

A few days later, while I was driving by her place, I saw the green Volkswagen bus again. *That fucking bus.* But I pretended that the situation didn't exist. Out of sight, out of mind. Except I saw the green bus again the next day. Then the next day I saw it again. Soon the green bus was parked outside her apartment every night. It became an open secret that everyone knew about, including me. But I just didn't want to accept it. I just wanted her to love me. I wanted her back.

I decided I was going to fight for what we once had. I was going to fight for love. I was going to win her back.

"For her birthday, we're going to go to her house and win her over with a song," I told Caleb, a friend in the theater department who I knew could play guitar.

"Of course, great idea," said Caleb. I loved his positivity. There was no judgmental scolding of "Kunal, dude, she's cheating on you, forget this witch." Everyone loved Grace—even then—and they understood why I wanted her back in my life.

So with Caleb and a few other friends, we practiced an a cappella version of "The Still of the Night." They took it really seriously, and we all rehearsed it like our life depended on it. Well, at this point, I really felt that my life did.

The plan: I would knock on the door to surprise her, we would start softly with doo-wops, and when the chorus kicked in, I would ask her to slow-dance with me on her front porch.

On the night of her birthday, we showed up at her doorstep. Parked in front, like always, was the green bus. I didn't care. At that moment I didn't care if he was inside the house with her. This was my chance to win back Grace, and no amount of tattoos could get in my way.

I knocked on the door.

She answered. I caught a glimpse of Jeff on the couch as she closed the door behind her.

"Listen," I said.

She stepped out onto the porch as the guys began . . .

Doo-wop dooby-doo
Doo-wop dooby-doo

"Dance with me," I said, not asking a question.

She wrapped her arms around me as the lyrics began to flow—

In the still of the night
I held you, held you tight . . .

We began to dance slowly, gently, tenderly. I ran my hands through her hair, and she turned to jelly. I could feel her tears on my neck. I could smell her Egyptian Musk.

I'm thinking *THIS IS FUCKING AWESOME*. Jeff and his green

bus could go take a shit somewhere; I just wanted Grace, for the rest of her life, to remember this moment.

She looked at me. "Thank you. I love you."

She went back inside and I can imagine that she probably cried some more, and Jeff probably held her, and then, later that night, they probably made love.

❖

Many weeks earlier, before the dance, before things had soured, I had offered to drive her to her parents' house when she graduated (a *six-hour* drive). Now we were broken up, but I didn't want to back out. I wanted to see her off. I felt like I owed it to her. Or maybe I just wanted to spend as much time with her as I could.

I helped her pack up all her stuff. We drove the six hours and when we arrived, her parents, whom I had met before, invited me to stay for dinner and the night. I accepted.

Grace and I slept in separate rooms (it *was* her parents' house), so when her folks went to bed I said good night to Grace, slipped on my pajamas, and went to sleep in the guest room. Tired from a long drive, I fell asleep instantly.

At 2 a.m. I heard a knock.

I know that knock.

I knew what was coming next.

"Koooooooooonel."

Wordlessly I opened the door.

Déjà vu.

"Come sit with me in the living room," she said.

I obliged.

We didn't talk. We had already done all the talking. Instead, right there on her parents' couch, boyfriend and girlfriend or not, we made love.

And as she closed her eyes and drifted off I remember studying her face. Her breathing was not so gentle anymore; she was no longer gently smiling. She had said good-bye already.

❖

The next morning it was actually time to say good-bye. For real this time. I opened the trunk of my car and threw in my bag.

"I love you. I'll miss you," she said.

"Same," I said, hopping in the car to drive off.

"Oh shit, I almost forgot!" she said.

My key was already in the ignition when she dashed into the house. She returned with a small brown sack. "I made you peanut butter and jelly sandwiches. I even cut the crusts off."

At the words "peanut butter" the floodgates opened and she began to cry. I hugged her through the car's window, accepted the sandwiches, and drove off. *I won't cry. I won't cry. I won't cry.*

I flipped on the car's stereo and inserted a CD.

True love waits on lollipops and crisps.
True love waits on lollipops and crisps.

I played the song on a loop for hours, and I bawled my eyes out. I mean it just gushed from me, tears upon tears upon tears. And then, hours later, after driving for hundreds of miles, something strange happened: I began to feel good. It was as if I had been cleansed. It was as if the poison of Saruman had washed away and the trees could grow again. I was free of the anxiety. Free of the jealousy. And I realized what I had known all along: the problem *really was me*, and that it was my fault for pushing her away. You see, love doesn't belong to anyone. You can't force it on someone and you can't take it away from someone. The more you try to hold on to it and keep it for yourself, the more fleeting it is.

Or maybe I just realized that I should have spotted a few red flags when I first connected with the girl of my dreams by licking her eyeball.

As I pulled into Portland I felt a lightness in my spirit. I looked at my phone and saw a name that intrigued me: Miyuki, a cute Japanese girl from school. Hmmm. I stopped for gas, and as the tank was filling I sat on the hood of my car eating an ice-cream cone, looking at the pink and mauve hue of the dusky sky. I flipped open my phone. "Hey, Miyuki, wanna hang tonight?"

❖

Music is fodder for my soul. Without it, I could not have gotten through heartbreak. I could not have traveled so far. I could never have loved the way I do now. Music taught me that. It eased my pain. It has been my lifeline.

The Prince and the Pauper

ONE GOOD THING CAME OUT OF MY BREAKUP WITH GRACE.
I lost a girlfriend, but I gained a band. Remember Caleb, who
helped me try to win Grace back? We started a two-man acoustic band called the Prince and the Pauper. I was the Prince (cuz I
called dibs), and Caleb was the Pauper (slower to call dibs).

Both Caleb and I were coming off an emotional time in our
lives. He too had just had a falling-out with a girl he loved, and we
bonded over our similar breakups. Also, we were in college in Portland, Oregon, which makes us legally obliged to sing weepy melancholy songs that can be best described as emo. *Emo* is basically
short for "emotional rock." We had the emotional part down.

Our very first tune, a little ditty about Grace, was titled "She's
Mine." It began:

> *I woke up this morn'*
> *Drenched in love potion and lipstick*

And then the chorus, wait for it:

> *She's mine*

She's mine
She's miiiiinne

Yup. Thaaaaaat kind of song. In retrospect our sound was Ra-diohead meets Justin Bieber. But, you know, in that moment it was the greatest song that we had ever sung, or that had *ever* been sung, because it was about Grace.

We played "She's Mine" on campus and it was a hit. By "hit," I mean that we played in front of thirty friends—an audience who would applaud even if we sang an off-key version of "Happy Birthday" in our tighty-whities. *But still.* People did sing along with the chorus.

She's mine
She's mine
She's miiiiiiiine

Let me tell you, when you have thirty people singing along to a song that you wrote, that's really all you need in life.

"Maybe we should take our show on the road?" Caleb said.

"Like play at . . . *real venues?*"

"Off-campus."

"Um. Okay. I'm in."

We started by scouring the paper for open mics in the greater Portland area. We were also writing more songs—six more songs, to be exact. Moody numbers that included gems like "So I'm Lonely Again" and "Misery" and "The Taste of Your Tears." We jammed hard. We practiced. Hard. We were serious.

We found a venue that seemed suitable for our world debut: a coffee shop called Java Bean. In fact it was across the street from where Dziko and I used to drink coffee and play chess, and they made an incredibly good coffee milk shake. We walked into the coffee shop and asked the manager, "Can we play music here?"

He looked at the two of us. Skeptical. "Do you have guitars?"

"Yes."

"All right, bring them in and play for me. Let's see what you've got."

"Right here?"

He shrugged as if to say, *Any better options?* And so, about thirty minutes later, we returned huffing and puffing from taking the bus all the way back to campus to get our guitars and stood right in the middle of the coffee shop, surrounded by the clanking of dishes and the hiss of the espresso machine. And we sang—

She's mine she's mine she's mine she's mine.

Silence.

The guy had a poker face.

Finally he said, "Not bad. Why don't you play on Thursday evening, say from five to seven?"

We felt like kings. We printed flyers announcing our show: "Prince and the Pauper: playing Emotional Love Acoustic Songs." We put them up all over the university, hoping to draw a big crowd, and of course we texted, emailed, and called all of our close friends.

On the day of the "concert" we felt like a *real* band. I wore torn jeans, a faded red Coca-Cola T-shirt, a white denim jacket, and yellow Converse sneakers. We were *Portlandia* before there was a show called *Portlandia.* We tuned our guitars and set up our mics, watching as our friends trickled into the small cafe. First just two or three. Then ten. Then fifteen. Then twenty. Then the cafe ran out of chairs. Then thirty. Soon the entire venue was packed with at least forty-five theater kids. Who cares if it was a crowd full of only our friends? It was a *crowd* nevertheless, and they were all there to see us.

"You good?" Caleb asked before we got onstage, and by "stage" I mean a little nook by the dessert display.

Hell yeah I'm good. Less than two years ago I was a nervous freshman who couldn't make friends or cook ramen noodles, and now I was about to serenade a roomful of groupies. I felt alive. To this day thinking of that moment gives me goose bumps. Too often we focus on the greater schemes in life, like making money, or getting promoted at work, or starting a new relationship—and yes, of course, those things matter—but sometimes it's the tiny, gradual, stepping-stone victories that bring real joy and signify the positive changes in our life.

We did a forty-minute set. I closed my eyes and just sang and sang and sang. There in the tiny Java Bean, I swear I could have died and all would have been all right. It was my Coachella. It was my Woodstock. We finished to thunderous applause. . . .

"ENCORE! ENCORE! ENCORE!" the crowd chanted.

Oh, you shouldn't have.

(And they sort of didn't. Caleb and I had asked a friend to start the encore chant.)

"No, no, no, we couldn't!" I said to the crowd.

"Good night, everyone!" said Caleb.

We were playing it to perfection.

"ENCORE! ENCORE! ENCORE!"

Caleb and I looked at each other—made a show of reluctantly

picking up our guitars, and then jumped right back in. *If the fans insist . . .* The crowd sang along as we began—

> *She's mine*
> *She's mine*
> *She's miiiine*

❖

After the success at Java Bean, we decided it was time to take it to the next level. Our heads were buzzing with excitement.

"We should record an album," I told Caleb.

"A real album?"

"An EP."

"Absolutely! I'm not sure what that is, but I'm in."

We found a guy to help us with the recording equipment, penned some new songs, and bunkered ourselves in a studio. By "guy" I mean my Hawaiian friend Cam, whose father was a famous ukulele player; Cam would record tunes for his father and send them to Hawaii. And by "studio" I mean his dorm room. Caleb sat on the top bunk, me on the bottom, Cam at his desk, and we laid down some tracks.

Afterward I played the first song back: *Ugh. That's what my voice sounds like?* I had never really heard myself sing, and I was bitterly disappointed. (I got over it quickly, though; Auto-Tune really is a wonderful thing.) And after nine hours in the recording studio, in a quiet room, in a not-so-quiet dorm, without the instant validation of applause, we stumbled onto a key lesson about making music: it is disgustingly hard work.

Finally, we slapped together a three-track demo and burned thirty copies onto discs. The plan was to play at venues and then sell the CDs at the show, which was the surefire path to gaining popularity and eventually a record deal.

But where would we play? How did we book concerts? Our only "venue" was the Java Bean, and while they did pay us in the form of free coffee and milk shakes, we realized we needed to step it up a notch.

We called bars all over Portland. For two months we weren't getting much response when finally, out of the blue, someone agreed to let us play: a dive bar called Sandy's in the suburbs of Beaverton, Oregon.

As we began printing out flyers for our first professional gig, it dawned on us that our entire "fan base" consisted of theater students who weren't even twenty-one yet; in fact, only three of the seniors could even get into the bar. We loaded up a van with our equipment and drove to Beaverton. We saw Sandy's at the end of a long dusty road. The parking lot was full of motorcycles and a few big trucks. My stomach began to churn.

We opened the door. The room smelled like piss and cigarettes and was filled with truckers and Hell's Angels.

"This is a bad idea," Caleb said.

Agreed. Nothing about that room said, *You know what? I'm in the mood for some emotional acoustic love songs!*

A woman of indeterminate age in a tight skirt skittered out from a dark corner and approached us. She looked like the slug boss monster from *Monsters, Inc.*, with skin that was shiny and vaguely green. An unlit cigarette dangled from her mouth. I had the vague sense that she carried a 9 mm pistol in her skirt. This was Sandy.

"Are you boys the Prince and the Pauper?" she asked in a voice that sounded like lung cancer.

We nodded meekly. *Oh God. How do we get out of here?*

"Are you going to get up and play?" Sandy asked.

Like prisoners lining up against the wall for a firing squad, we glumly set up our equipment on the small stage. The bar was dark and musty and the carpet looked like a giant Scottish kilt. Our three loyal friends from school sat in the front row, which was also the *only* row of seats; the other dozen truckers and bikers sat at the bar, with their backs to us.

"Hey, everybody," Sandy said, pausing only to cough up a lung, "this is the Prince and the Pauper. Put your hands together and enjoy."

No applause. No one turned around. A few halfhearted claps from our friends, who were fearing for their lives.

"A one, a two, a one two three . . ." and I began our first number:

> *So I'm lonely again.*
> *So I'm looooonnnnnnneely again.*

Kill me. Mostly I kept my eyes on the floor, peeking up to see that none of the truckers had turned around. They completely blocked us out, as if we were that annoying sound of a dying mosquito, or they were all deaf from riding motorcycles all day. Sandy stood in the corner, staring at us, an unblinking statue, smoking her life away.

"Dude, let's just play one more song," I said to Caleb.

> *She's mine she's mine she's mine*

We got some applause from our three friends and no one else.

"Thanks, guys, for listening," I said into the mic. "It's been a great night."

I began to unplug the guitar.

"You said an hour!" called out Sandy from the back of the bar.

"Ah, I think maybe—"

"Play more. Play more stuff."

Shit. Either these guys are going to shoot us because they hate our music, or she's going to shoot us for not finishing our set. With the fear of death in our eyes, we staggered through another few songs, quickly packed up, and limped our way out of the bar.

Sandy walked out to our van behind us, creeping slowly on our heels. *What does she want?*

"You did a good job up there," she said, cracking a warm but toothless smile. "You have potential. But if you guys want to play here again, you need to practice more."

What the hell? She's *giving us notes?*

After escaping with our lives, we decided that would be our final outside gig. No more leaving the bubble of college. We played again at the Java Bean, and of course we jammed at all our after parties, but soon we realized that maybe, just maybe, we should focus on something that better suited our skill set, like, say, acting. And we realized something about our groupie friends. They weren't actual groupies. All of them came out to support our band's *first* show, and 80 percent of them came out to support our second show, then maybe 50 percent came to our third, and after that, we were on our own.

But who knows. Maybe someday Caleb and I will get the band back together. Only a few days ago he sent me an old recording he found of us. And you know what? It wasn't half as bad as I thought.

After hearing the recording, I picked up my guitar and started strumming. I thought—

Maybe Portland just wasn't ready for the Prince and the Pauper.

Are you?

SO I'M LONELY AGAIN

A song by the Prince and the Pauper. Key "E." 4/4.

So I'm lonely again
So I'm lonely again
Walking back from your house Sunday
Couldn't help but see
That your eyes reflected of last night
And the passion between you and me
I note I was barely breathing
Did you feel the same
If you did are we heading for something
These trustful eyes have never seen
So, I, so I'm lonely again
So I'm lonely again
I heard that games weren't your forte
Then why am I made of glass
All my friends lie when they tell me
You lose
You looooose
Between night and day
Our differences lay
Between night and day
Our differences lay

How I Knew

CABARET WOULD BE MY BREAKTHROUGH. I COULD SENSE that my time had come. As a sophomore, I had been around the theater group long enough to make some pretty good friends, and when the prior year's seniors graduated, naturally I was that much higher on the pecking order. And I could sing! (Or so I thought.) *Cabaret* is a musical, and I had been training for this role since birth.

When I was growing up, we would spend our summers in a charming little town at the foothills of the Himalayas. And every summer the community hosted these kiddie talent competitions for all the visiting families. When I was eight, I entered my first competition and lip-synched Billy Joel's "We Didn't Start the Fire," which I accompanied with my version of a break dance. Which basically meant intensely shaking my body from head to toe, almost like a convulsion. My mother gave me some performance advice: *Don't forget to acknowledge the crowd after you're done, Kunal.* I didn't really know what that meant, but after I finished the song I strutted away from the crowd, slowly, then turned my head back to them, and gave them a salute. The crowd went nuts and I won second place. (First place went to this creepy kid who made balloon animals. He made me a balloon duck to commemorate our friendship.)

After the talent show, music became a big part of my life. My dad had a dusty old guitar in storage and I found it, cleaned it up, and decided to make it my best friend. I bought a pictorial guide to chords and basically taught myself how to play the guitar. The first song I learned was Poison's "Every Rose Has Its Thorn." Next came Extreme's "More than Words." I even became obsessed with hip-hop, watching MTV and practicing the moves the artists did in their videos. At the time MTV had just come on cable and I would religiously watch the show *The Grind*, which was basically a big hip-hop pool party that would play music videos and then cut to real girls dancing by the pool in bikinis. At a young age I learned how to drop it like it was hot.

You can say I had garnered some confidence in my voice and in my dancing, and after the *Ring Around the Moon* fiasco, I had enrolled in acting classes so my acting skills, too, were beginning to take shape. When I auditioned for the lead in *Cabaret*, the part of the emcee, I had a feeling that it could go my way. During the audition, they kept asking me to stay after most of the other actors left, and it basically came down to me and my roommate Ben.

Ben had an absolutely beautiful voice, and he *really* looked the part. *Cabaret* is a musical set in 1930s Germany during the early days of the Nazi regime, and let's just say there weren't a lot of brown people running around Berlin in those days. So I comforted myself with the thought, *Well, even if I don't get the lead, I'll still get to be in the chorus.* After a long audition I went to sleep, exhausted and exhilarated.

The next morning I raced over to the theater to look at the cast list. I searched for my name at the top, eager to see the sign that would boldly proclaim in thirty-point font:

THE UNIVERSITY OF PORTLAND IS PROUD TO PRESENT A PRODUCTION OF *CABARET,* STARRING, AS THE EMCEE, KUNAL NAYYAR!!!!

Then I looked at the actual sign . . . Ben Van Diepen cast as the emcee. I began to scroll down with my finger. I kept scrolling and scrolling until I reached the bottom of the list.

"That's odd," I actually said out loud. I rescanned the list, searching for my name, and a swell began to form deep in my gut. *I am not on the list. Anywhere. I don't have the lead part. I'm not a supporting character. I'm not in the chorus. I'm not an extra.* There were forty students in the theater program and this play had thirty-eight parts. I was one of only two actors who got *nothing.*

I left the lobby in a huff. I wanted people to see me mad. I wished my middle finger was a machine gun so I could shoot fuck-yous at everyone there. Not even an *extra.* They didn't even want to see my face onstage. *My brown face.* At first I thought I didn't get cast because of my ethnicity. That was a defense mechanism I had created for myself—an easy way to explain failure when it didn't make sense to me—but that's a dangerous path to go down. We all do that to ourselves. Explain *irrationally* the rational. We make up stories in our heads instead of looking at the facts. We force perse-cution on ourselves when there is none. The truth is simple. I. Just. Wasn't. Good. Enough.

I was suddenly alone. Again. Thirty-eight of the forty theater students were cast in that play—spending all their evenings to-gether, rehearsing, making new inside jokes. I was back to square one. When it was time for *Cabaret*'s opening night I decided to not even show up to watch. It was stupid and naïve, I know, but I was hurting, and I was behaving like a child. I *did* want to see it. I did want to support Ben and all my friends. So, I sucked it up and decided to attend closing night. But during the performance I couldn't help but think, *How am I not a part of this?*

❖

Cut to: junior year. The summer is over. Wounds have healed. Time for a new semester and a new play. The play was *The Rose Tattoo*, by Tennessee Williams. I had my eye on the role of Alvaro Mangia-cavallo, an Italian truck driver. And *obviously* I'm Italian-looking.* I memorized my lines and said them in the shower every morning. I read the play in its entirety twice, highlighting and scribbling notes, then wrote a long bio of the character. This was the first time as an actor that I was 100 percent prepared. And now, as a junior, I also had the benefit of additional acting classes. More important, though, I had a newfound appreciation of how hard I needed to work, and what it was really going to take to achieve my ultimate goal of getting the lead.

I lived and breathed Alvaro and thought about him from every angle. Let's take his physicality: He's a truck driver, right? That probably means he's sitting down a lot because he's driving the damn truck all the time, so when he gets up from a chair, he might have just the slightest amount of back pain. It's barely noticeable but it adds texture. (As compared to, say, my 117-year-old butler, who walked like Gandalf.) If this truck driver saw a beautiful woman,

---

* Actually this really was an edge: I was probably the closest thing our school had to Sicilian.

what would his first reaction be? Maybe his first instinct is to cower, which would result in his overcompensating with an even more inflated show of bravado. How would he drink his water? I obsessed over how he gripped a pen, how long he held eye contact, how he would take a leak. I'd never worked this hard for *Cabaret* or *Ring Around the Moon* or badminton or my band or for anything, really.

"The part is yours," the director told me right after the audition. There would be no waiting for the casting sheet. I was silently elated. For the first time in my life I thought, *Hey, maybe there actually* is *a future in this whole acting thing.*

❖

For the play I was supposed to have an Italian accent. But in real life, I actually have an Indian accent. And though I tried to master the Italian accent, onstage the two accents would sometimes blur, and I would go back and forth between Italian and Indian. But what I learned was that if you're completely committed to the character, it doesn't really matter if sometimes you botch an accent.* The audience isn't thinking about what you look like or sound like. Truth is, if they can tell that *you* believe your character's journey with every cell of your being, they'll always be on your side.

And thankfully, they were on my side. Opening night treated us to thunderous applause, then the same with the second performance, then the third, and it became apparent that we would likely get nominated for ACTF again. Then I heard some buzz that I, personally, could get an acting nomination for ACTF.

Thursday night. Our fourth performance. Something happened during that performance that would change the course of

---

* Some would disagree.

my life. It would be the one acting moment that ultimately led me to become the guy who's writing this book. There's a scene when my character, Alvaro, through various hijinks and follies, finds himself at a widow's house, and he explains to her (in an Italian/Indian accent, of course) that he had never felt silk on his skin.

The widow, Serafina, walks into the closet and pulls out a red shirt. She offers it to Alvaro.

Serafina: Nothing's too good for the man if the man is good.

Alvaro: The grandson of a village idiot is not that good.

Serafina: No matter whose grandson you are, put it on; you are welcome to wear it. [She gives him the shirt.]

This had always been one of my favorite scenes, but that night, for some reason, something was different. It felt like there was no audience; that no one was watching. As if the only two people that mattered in that moment were Alvaro and Serafina. When she handed me that shirt and I slipped it over my head, it felt like my entire body was melting into the silk. Like the way you snuggle back into a blanket on a cold Monday morning. I *felt* something. I felt *truth*. The shirt wasn't actually made of silk; it was a college play and budgets were small. But it could have been anything; in that moment it *was* silk, and I was wearing it for the very first time. As I sank into the shirt I released a sound from my mouth, like a silent *s*, a barely audible *sssssssssssss*. I had never made that sound in rehearsal or during the play. I don't know where it came from. I made that sound and the entire audience—at least in my mind's ears—all exhaled audibly, in unison. Just one collective deep breath.

And I began to cry. In that moment the character of Alvaro is not supposed to cry, but I was having an out-of-body experience. Tears flowed down my cheeks. I suppose someone might say that by crying I took the character out of the scene and did a disservice to the play, but I could tell—I could *feel*—that the audience was with me. Completely, utterly with me. And I wasn't crying because the character was feeling silk on his skin for the first time; I was crying because I finally got it. I was crying because I now understood that this is what I wanted to do for the rest of my life. I was crying because I realized how much heartache it took to get here. And I was crying because I knew that I had the power to control the energy in the room.

After that performance I went home, and I replayed that moment in my mind, and I kept hearing over and over again, *sssssssssss.* It made me realize the audience really *is* on my side. I had found something inside myself that made me *believe.* It was time to let go of the fear. Before I was my own worst enemy—the self-doubt, the insecurity—and now I could break free of those shackles. After that *sssssssssss* I knew that something had changed. *I get it now. I'm in.*

The next day I called my mom and dad.

"I'm not going to business school," I told them. "I've decided I want to be an actor."

"How are you going to pay your bills?" they could have said.

"It's a tough industry, this is a bad idea," they could have said.

"We invested so much to get you over there, don't blow it," they could have said.

"That's great. Proud of you!" they actually said.

I love them for that answer.

In the very next performance I tried to re-create the moment.

The widow gave me the red silk shirt, I slipped it on and said *sssssssssss*, and waited for the magic. Nothing happened. No tears. No snuggling into a warm blanket on a cold Monday morning. Nothing. The night after that I tried again. Nothing. Every night I tried to feel the same magic. Nothing. It was a once-in-a-lifetime moment. Everything I needed to learn from that moment, I had learned. It showed me the path to my future. But now the moment had passed. I am not sure the audience could tell the difference; I felt that they were still with me every night during that scene. But for me, I couldn't re-create the same magic within. That happens in life, where a brief, fleeting moment can change us forever, and as hard as we try, it cannot be re-created. And just as hard as it is to re-create, it is harder yet to let it go. To this day, after all my acting endeavors, I have never been able to re-create what I felt that night. Maybe that is the dream I am really chasing. That and an Oscar.

❖

The Rose Tattoo did get nominated for ACTF, so we boarded a plane and returned to my old stomping grounds of Boise, Idaho. We were back in the same hotel, we performed on the same stage, and we were about to get adjudicated by the same crusty old gargoyles.

This year, though, things were different. I now had actual friends and no longer had to quarantine myself in my hotel room; in fact, *I* had the beers in my room and invited people to join me. I had graduated from Mike's Hard Lemonade to actual beer. I still remember how lonely I had felt as a freshman, so I threw hotel parties that brought everyone together—all my friends from Portland, even strangers from all the other theater programs. I finally felt like I belonged. That year was also different because I was nominated individually as an actor, and I would be competing against actors from twenty-five different colleges. I had to perform a monologue against four hundred other competitors. Based on these monologues, the adjudicators would send two of us to Washington, D.C., for the nationals.

I performed the "Tangled Up in Blue" monologue from the play by Brad Boesen of the same name:

. . . You asked me why I never stayed very long with the women I've dated; it's you. Because of you. Because I didn't want to settle anymore. I've been doing it all my life, and I didn't want to settle. . . .

And every woman I met, every one, I would compare them to you, and they weren't you. They just weren't. And I refused to settle until . . . until I knew one way or another.

So don't tell me that I'm just drunk, or that I don't really feel the way I feel, because I've had four years to think about this, and I know how I feel.

It wasn't quite the *sssssssssss* moment, but I still felt really good about my performance.

But what about those gargoyle adjudicators?

After all of us had finished our monologues, and after the applause faded and the crowd thinned from the auditorium, once again, as before, we changed out of our costumes and patiently awaited our judgment.

The doors to the auditorium opened. The judges entered. They looked just as I remembered: these ancient pillars of pretension, all of them bearded, all of them wearing suspenders. They looked like Santa Claus if the role of Santa Claus was being played by Satan. I imagined that when they opened their mouths they would breathe fire. Were they the same judges as before? Maybe, I don't know— all white people look alike to me.*

"I have a question about your monologue's . . . realism," I imagined the first judge saying, looking at his notes. "Would you really speak that way to a girl, COOONEL?"

Or maybe a judge would look at his notes, adjust his glasses, and say, "I know from your *words* that you were speaking to a girl, but for me, I couldn't *feel* that girl."

Or perhaps a third would say, "Your Indian accent just wasn't believable."

But what actually happened was this. One of the evil Santa Clauses looked at his notes, looked at me, pronounced my name correctly, and said, "Kunal, when you are able to make every person in the audience collectively release an audible *awwww* in unison, you've achieved something very special. Congratulations."

I was headed to D.C. for nationals.

---

* This is not a joke. All white people really do look the same. To me.

Kunal's Twelve Quick Thoughts on Dating

1. MEN SHOULD USE THE WORD *ADORABLE*.

Women love it when men say words like *adorable*, ideally in an adorable accent. Here is a list of word substitutes that women find charming.

If you like something—call it adorable.

If you think someone is pretty—tell her she's gorgeous.

If you want to talk about your bowels—always use the word *poop*.

Don't say you like sex—say you like making love.

Use these words early and often—*moral ineptitude, primarily, morality,* and *lovely.*

2. BE HONEST.

But not too honest. Don't tell her too much. On the first date, you don't have to tell her about the time you went skinny-dipping with your mom. But do tell her that you like skinny-dipping in general.

3. WHEN IN DOUBT, ASK QUESTIONS.

This always works. Always. Whenever the date is going poorly just start asking questions. For example, "How do you feel about kissing on a first date?"

4. NEVER DISCUSS POLITICS.

Because liberals and conservatives have traditionally never enjoyed having sex with each other.

5. YOU CAN KEEP IT SIMPLE.

I never understood why men couldn't just go up to a girl, ask her name, ask if she was having a good time, where she was from, and if she would like a drink. Instead, they opt for something like this: Walk close enough to a group of girls, order a round of shots, and say, "Yo, son, let's get a round of lemon drops and drop it like it's hot; where the honeys tonight, y'all?"

I'll tell you where the honeys are tonight, my friend: they are hanging out with guys who don't sound like you.

6. DON'T BE LATE.

That is not cool. Ever.

7. THE MAN SHOULD PAY.

It's just the way that I was raised. I once went on a date with a woman who was nine years older than me, and we went to a French creperie. The bill was $28.06. She seemed really into women's rights and I was trying to be all progressive-like, so we split the bill exactly down the middle and each paid $14.03. Not impressive. If you are going to split the bill on a date, at least round it to the nearest integer.

8. DON'T WAIT TWO DAYS TO CALL SOMEONE BACK.

I know every single advice column in the world says "Wait two days," but if you wait two days, to me, that means that I'm not important to you. So why wait?

9. ALWAYS MAKE THE EFFORT.

Don't be afraid to bring flowers because of how you're going to be perceived. I've never met a woman who didn't appreciate flowers. In fact, I'm a man and if you brought me a bouquet, I would be impressed.

10. NEVER FALL FOR THOSE PEOPLE SELLING ROSES.

You know those guys who come by your table and try to sell you roses? Yeah, it's a scam. One night on a date, while maybe a little drunk, I paid a hundred dollars to buy the entire bouquet. Why?

1. I felt bad for the guy working so late on a Saturday night.

2. I thought if I bought the entire bouquet he could stop work for the night and go home to his family.

3. I really wanted to impress my date.

4. Maybe I was a *lot* drunk.

Not ten minutes later, *the same guy came back with an entirely new bouquet!* The ass-clown's car was parked just down the street. He was driving an Audi. Three Series. The Audi was full of flowers.

He bought that car on the tears of all the men he had duped into buying those damn roses. Me included.

11. MANNERS MATTER.

Don't smack your lips when you eat. And girls, when we open the door for you, don't say, "Why are you doing that, do you think I'm too weak—because I'm a *woman*—to open the door myself?" We're just trying to be polite.

12. CALL HER "DUDE."

If all else fails, call a woman "dude," repeatedly. It will confuse her, it'll throw her equilibrium off balance, her mind will be blown, and she will sleep with you.

Holiday Traditions Part 3: Holi

Holi (*HO-lee*): ***n.*** Indian holiday known as the
Festival of Colors or the Festival of Love.

HOLI CELEBRATES . . . WELL, ACTUALLY, I DON'T REALLY KNOW
what it celebrates, maybe something about good and evil, but it's
my favorite Indian festival because basically it is when people get
together and drink bhang, which is hash in liquid form, and get
high as kites. Then we smear each other with dry colored powder
and shoot each other in the face with water cannons.

India is always a very colorful country, but Holi is India on ste-
roids. It's an insanely raucous occasion in every city, on every block,
a party with frequent, startling, wet explosions of red and yellow
and green. You can't leave your home without getting soaked from
head to toe with color.

We fought Holi wars (ha) with our neighbors, and I was always a big wussy. One year I tried to sneak up on the neighborhood bully with some guerrilla warfare tactics, lying low on the
ground behind him, and when he turned around I squirted him in
the face. . . . His eyes grew wide as he revealed a huge water balloon
he had been saving to hit me with. He pelted that damn balloon

at me, hitting me right on the nose and blasting green all over my face. I ran all the way home screaming and crying.

"Look at what he did to my face!" I sobbed to my mother, which is hilarious because *everyone's* face was smeared with color.

"What a crybaby," she said laughing.

She was right.

Holi (*HO-lee*): *n.* 1. Indian holiday known as the Festival of Colors or the Festival of Love. 2. Unofficially, the eve of India's national day of laundry.

Nina, Why?

WHEN YOU FINISH COLLEGE AND YOU'RE CRAZY ENOUGH TO want to be an actor, you basically have four options:

1. Move to New York and start working.

2. Move to Los Angeles and start working.

3. Stay in your current city and start working.

4. Go to graduate theater school.

I would have chosen options 1, 2, and 3 in a heartbeat, but truthfully, I just didn't feel like I had all the skills it would take to be a professional actor. So I chose option 4. I needed to get better. In the ACTF nationals I had won a couple of awards and caught the interest of a pretty good agent and I felt that I could do a couple of things well. I believed I had a decent command over my comedic timing, but found it hard to connect sometimes with scenes that required me to dig deep and access my emotions. I wanted to expand my range as an actor. I was worried I would become a one-trick pony. I needed to add more tools to my bag.

So when I was a senior I flew to Chicago, where at the downtown Hilton hotel I would spend an entire weekend of ball-busting auditions for grad school. By analogy, these are roughly equivalent to an NFL draft combine, where the nation's top recruits throw footballs and run routes and wind sprints for NFL scouts, and if you flub your workout you won't get drafted. Except in this one you have *three minutes* to perform.

You perform for three minutes onstage in front of a crowd of forty-six people. Every person in that crowd is the head of a graduate theater department. And in those three minutes, actually, you perform a ninety-second comedic monologue and a ninety-second dramatic monologue. That's it. If you perform for three minutes and one second, you're disqualified and you can kiss grad school good-bye. You so much as blink and it's over.

For my comedic piece I played Moth from *Love's Labour's Lost*, and for my dramatic piece I stuck with what had served me well at ACTF—*Tangled Up in Blue*. It seemed obvious to play to my strengths. I'm always baffled when actors choose to audition with a monologue where they play a rapist, or a child molester, or a serial killer. Or pick a monologue where they spend the entire time screaming at the audience. Why wouldn't they pick something that makes them likable? After all, these theater schools are investing in you for three years, so you don't really want to scare them away.

Casey, the brightest star of our theater program, did her auditions a little before me.

"I sucked, I sucked, I sucked," she said when she came back to the hotel room.

"I'm sure you didn't suck," I said.

She handed me an envelope. *The* envelope. This envelope gives you the entire list of schools that liked your monologues and want to interview you. There are forty-six schools total. Casey was a talented actress, so I guessed that she would be selected by at least seven schools, maybe eight or nine. (Personally, I would have been happy with five.)

Casey showed me the envelope and I saw . . . one. Only one school wanted to interview her. *Are you kidding me?* She was such a wonderful actress. I had looked up to her throughout college.

"Kunal, you're up," someone told me.

I made my way to the stage, trying to ignore the fact that this was easily the most important three minutes of my life. I remembered what my mother had told me as a child: *Acknowledge the crowd, Kunal.* I knew that the second I said a word they would start the clock and my three minutes would begin, so instead, before I started speaking, I took a long, deep breath, and I smiled a big smile at the audience. This was my way of letting them know that I was happy to be there. That I appreciated the moment.

After my audition, I sat outside nervously awaiting the envelope. It had gone well, I thought. A few minutes went by. I swear I could hear the tick-tock of my wristwatch. Then I heard my name and an old professorial-looking lady handed me a white, legal-size envelope with my name on it. I stared at it, terrified to open it, feeling that sucker punch of anxiety that every high school student experiences when they open the mailbox to find a letter of acceptance (or rejection) from college. I went into the bathroom of the Hilton to open it alone.*

---

* Which was very brave of me, as I hate public bathrooms and only use them under extreme duress. I've just never understood the concept of people pooping next to each other.

I opened the envelope.

Twelve schools wanted to interview me.

Yes!

Shit.

Yes!

Shit.

The good news was that twelve schools is a lot of schools; the bad news was that it was *so many* interviews—all back-to-back-to-back—so as a matter of pure logistics, it would be difficult to attend all the interviews at the hotel without being late. And I'm never late. So with a pen and paper, I drew up a floor plan of the hotel and figured out how I could use the emergency stairwells to avoid the crowds at elevators and optimize all the routes. (Raj would have been proud.)

I made every interview on time. I was most impressed with Temple University, a school that only accepted eight students once every three years.

If I was accepted, it would mean that I would live in Philadelphia, which is close to New York and might give me a shot at Broadway. *If* I was accepted, it would mean a full-ride scholarship. *If* I was accepted, it would give me another guaranteed three years in America.

I was accepted.

And then I wasn't.

In the same week I received two very different phone calls. The first began, "Kunal, congratulations, Temple University would like to extend an offer of admission."

Then the second call came.

"Kunal, there's a problem."

"Okay."

"The university is not allowed to give a scholarship to anyone with a GPA below a 3.3."

"But my GPA *is* 3.3," I said.

"Your GPA is 3.26."

❖

I had done enough math to know that 3.3 − 3.26 = .04, which is essentially a rounding error, a number so small, so arbitrary, that it's the difference of *one class* being a B instead of a B-plus. I pleaded with Temple's admissions department—and after two painstaking weeks of groveling they finally said, "If you write a personal letter to the dean of the university, maybe they will take that into consideration."

So I wrote an over-the-top emotional appeal, saying that the reason I didn't have a higher GPA was that I was also a business student, juggling two course loads, taking marketing classes all day and then theater at night. This was the truth. None of the other theater students was doing that. Besides, what did my C in Portfolio Risk Analysis have to do with an ability to play Moth? I had an A in all my *acting* classes, and I was applying to *acting* school. I explained all of this in the letter, and laced it with about a thousand "pretty pleases."

The letter did the trick, or maybe it was the "pretty pleases"; either way, they waived the GPA requirement and accepted me. (Takeaway: It's not over even when they say it's over. Always write the letter. Always appeal to a human to render a final judgment. We *are* human, after all.)

So, I had made it, right? I had been accepted into one of the most prestigious acting programs in the world. No more feeling like an outsider. No more feeling insecure. No more fretting about not getting the lead roles. Or getting roles at all. I had finally made it.

Or had I?

The first opportunity was our production of *Romeo & Juliet*. I was so fired up. Now, finally, I would have the chance to play Romeo. This time I wouldn't just be the comedic sidekick—I could show my dramatic chops. I've always wanted to play Romeo. For years I would whisper these words under my breath.

> *She speaks:*
> *O, speak again, bright angel! for thou art*
> *As glorious to this night, being o'er my head*
> *As is a winged messenger of heaven*
> *Unto the white-upturned wondering eyes*
> *Of mortals that fall back to gaze on him*
> *When he bestrides the lazy-pacing clouds*
> *And sails upon the bosom of the air.*

I only had one competitor for the role, a guy named Mike. The director auditioned us both in the same room at the same time, having us read the very same lines. It was awkward.

"Kunal, now you read."

O, speak again, bright angel!

"Mike, your turn."

O, speak again, bright angel!

It was almost like kissing your girlfriend while she's also kissing her ex-boyfriend in the same room and trying to choose between the two of you. But it didn't really matter. I knew I had the stronger read. I had whispered those words thousands of times. I was Romeo.

The next day I walked up to the casting sheet and saw "Romeo . . . Mike."

Here we go again.

It was *Cabaret* all over again. Had nothing changed? I was angry with the director, angry with Mike, angry with Temple, angry with the whole goddamn world. I stormed out of the theater, just as I did a few years before. I wanted everyone to see me mad.

It's amazing how we continue to make the same mistakes in life over and over again. We repeat the same cycles of failure, long after we should have learned the lesson. Once again I resorted to my old defense mechanisms: *They didn't want a brown Romeo.* I secretly accused Mike of stealing all my choices in the audition. I questioned the entire premise of Temple—the whole reason I'm here is to grow as an actor, so why not let me grow by playing Romeo?

They ultimately cast me as Benvolio, and even though he is one of the male leads, I still took this as an insult. *You don't see me as the good-looking lothario, you see me as the funny second banana.* It stung. Always the jilted bridesmaid, that's me.

I did everything I could do to be the best Benvolio possible; I wanted *everyone* to know I was the harder-working actor. I mean, I supported Mike and the rest of the cast and I rooted for the play's success. But it wasn't easy. The jealousy boiled in my blood. Every rehearsal I watched Mike give his lines and I thought, *I care about this so much more than you do.* Every day was a struggle.

There's one speech in particular that Romeo gives to Friar Laurence:

> *But Romeo may not; he is banished:*
> *Flies may do this, but I from this must fly:*
> *They are free men, but I am banished.*

And say'st thou yet that exile is not death?
Hadst thou no poison mix'd, no sharp-ground knife,
No sudden mean of death, though ne'er so mean,
But "banished" to kill me?—"banished"?
O friar, the damned use that word in hell;
Howlings attend it: how hast thou the heart,
Being a divine, a ghostly confessor,
A sin-absolver, and my friend profess'd,
To mangle me with that word "banished"?

I had always dreamt of giving that speech. When Mike rehearsed those lines I caught myself mouthing along with him, repeating the word *banished* over and over. Sometimes I said the word at night in my bed, stressing different syllables.

> *Banish-ed*
> *Ban-is-hed*
> *Bani-shed*

❖

Luckily I had something to take my mind off all the perceived injustice. After class one day I got a call from that same agent I had met at ACTF, who said, "There's going to be a Broadway musical based on Bollywood."

"Really? Who's doing it?"

"Andrew Lloyd Webber and A. R. Rahman. They're doing a musical called *Bombay Dreams*, and I think you would be great as the lead."

C'mon, *the lead*?

Well, they needed someone who was Indian and funny, so at the very least I had one out of two. But they also needed someone who could sing. (I wonder if they'd heard about a promising little band called the Prince and the Pauper?)

The audition was in New York, so I took the seventeen-dollar Peter Pan bus from Philly to the Port Authority bus terminal, sitting right next to the driver because, according to urban legend, a guy once got decapitated in the back of a Peter Pan bus. The audition had two components: doing some scenes from the play, and then singing a song. Any song. I chose Billy Joel's "She's Got a Way," because obviously my finger was on the pulse of modern pop culture.

"*She's got a waaaaaaaaayyyyy.*" I sang that first note, and immediately the casting director snapped her head up, looking at me.

Is that a good sign or a bad sign? No idea. But I kept singing. I belted my little heart out, going all *American Idol*–like.

Then I read the sides and did my funny Indian thing.

"Who *are* you? How come I've never seen you before?" the casting director asked.

"I'm Kunal Nayyar and I am a graduate student at Temple University."

"Come with me."

❖

The casting director led me to her office and said she liked what she had heard, pumped me with self-confidence, and told me to come back in two weeks for callbacks for the lead role. The lead role! *Go fuck yourself, Romeo.*

Back at Temple I spent the next two weeks practicing the main song in the show, blasting Bollywood lyrics at the top of my lungs. Somewhere in my mind I was having Bombay dreams of my own. I sang that song again and again, sixteen hours a day. I knew it cold.

I can still sing it in my sleep. I sang that song so much that even my classmates caught themselves singing along—

The journey home
Is never too looooooong

Once again I took the Peter Pan bus to New York. Once again I somehow avoided decapitation. I returned to the audition studio and I sang for all the big-shot music directors.

"The journey home . . ."

They listened with poker faces.

"Is never too looooooong."

Afterward they said, "Great song, great song. Can you do some sides now?"

I did my lines and I *killed them.* The directors and producers were cracking up laughing. They gave me warm handshakes and said they would soon be in touch. I floated away from that audition. I took a walk through Central Park, enjoying the crisp February air and visualizing my future on Broadway. I sipped a hot chocolate and gazed at the skyline. *This is the life I want. I'm going to be a star.*

I stared at the phone and waited for it to ring.

It didn't ring.

I stared harder.

It didn't ring.

Finally the phone rang: I didn't get the part.

I would like to say, "You get used to these disappointments," but that would be a lie. It always hurts. It feels the same whether you're auditioning for a fifth-grade pageant or *Cabaret* in college or *Romeo & Juliet* in grad school or a Broadway show or a blockbuster Hollywood movie. The stage might be different, but if you care and you've invested all of yourself in the audition, the stakes are the same.

Back at grad school, I had another chance to prove that I could be a dramatic leading man: our school would do *The Seagull*, a Chekhov play. One of my favorite plays of all time. I had known that this would be our next play and I was eyeing the lead role of Kostya. I also felt that after Romeo didn't go my way, and after some of the other actors had already had the opportunity to play the lead in various plays, I would be asked to play Kostya. But nothing in life is ever handed to us, is it?

"Kunal, you're going to be Dr. Dorn," my acting teacher said.

"But we haven't even had auditions!"

"This is just the way I see it. You'll be a great Dorn."

Dorn is yet another physical-comedy guy. Not the leading man.

"Will you at least allow me to *read* for the part of Kostya?"

"No. This is how I see it."

We eventually agreed on a compromise for the "audition": as we read through the play as a group in the first act I would read the part of Dorn, and in the second act I would read for my coveted role of Kostya.

So I read Dr. Dorn in the first act (and maybe sucked a bit on purpose), then did my best version of Kostya. When we finished, our acting teacher said that he wouldn't reveal the casting just yet, because he had something to think about.

The next day I raced to the theater to read the cast list:

"Kunal Nayyar. Dorn."

How many times in my life would I need to prove myself? Once again I imagined these ridiculous scenarios, such as, maybe, the other guy made some side deal with our teacher.

But then I did what I had gotten so used to doing. *I worked.* I was determined to prove to everyone—and myself—that I was the hardest-working one in the room. I'd come to see that my work was the only piece of the whole enterprise that I could control.

In *The Seagull*, there's a scene in the third act where Kostya begins to go crazy. He grabs onto the woman he loves and he says, "Nina, why? Nina, why?" He keeps saying *Nina, why? Nina, why? Nina! Nina!*

Every night during that scene in the third act, I would go to the wings of the stage, and behind the big black curtain there was a little nook where I would sit. I would lean against the back walls of the theater. Inches from the stage, but just hidden enough so the audience couldn't see me. And when Kostya said, "Nina, why?" I would say those words, too. I would mouth along, dreaming that one day, I too would get to say them. I can still hear them like music, like a violin.

But the notes to that violin have changed. *Nina, why?* Over time I began to make sense out of the disappointment. For years I felt slighted and cheated when I was denied a shot at the "lead dramatic role." I felt like I was just doing more of the same. Always comedy, comedy, comedy. *Nina, why?* But what if I wasn't getting stereotyped? What if, instead, I was sharpening my comedic strengths? What if these teachers saw something in me, something that I was good at, and they wanted me to work harder and get better? And what if I was just being a sulky brat, and maybe those other guys were simply better than I in those particular parts?

Nina, why? I'll tell you why, Nina. Maybe my role as Benvolio wasn't a waste. Maybe it taught me a new mannerism or a quirk or it improved some aspect of my timing. Maybe my time as Dorn, which I accepted so ungratefully, gave me the confidence to later add more texture to a character named, say, Rajesh Koothrappali.

Listen up, Nina. This is important. If, in a parallel universe, I had been given the chance to play Romeo and Kostya, maybe, years later, agents wouldn't have seen me in a comedic light, and I would never have gotten to play shy little nerd Raj in the not-so-little show *The Big Bang Theory*, and I wouldn't be sitting here writing this book.

I was reminded of something important that my father had taught me all those years ago: *If it happens, good. If it doesn't happen, very good.*

A Thought Recorded on an
Aeroplane Cocktail Napkin

When you regift a bottle of
wine, Don't give it to the people
who gifted you that bottle in
the first place.

Love's Labour's Lost

WASHINGTON, D.C. A NEW CITY, A NEW APARTMENT, AND A new world. I was twenty-five and had just finished graduate school. I arrived in the capital with two suitcases stuffed with everything I owned.

I had just been cast in an Indian version of Shakespeare's *Love's Labour's Lost*, helmed by legendary director Michael Kahn. For the non-theater-folk out there, to paraphrase Ron Burgundy, Michael Kahn "is a pretty big deal." Was I the lead role? Nope. Supporting? Nope. I didn't have any lines, I was an understudy, and my itty-bitty role as a "minion" just meant, basically, that my only job was to carry mango milk shakes across the stage without spilling them. The play was crap. (Sorry, Michael.) It was so bad, and I felt bad for the actors because everyone was trying so hard. My character only existed for "Indian authenticity." It was borderline racist, even though I'm sure the intentions were pure enough. (It's the equivalent of eating fried chicken with a black person and telling them how much you admire their culture because of their ability to use a deep fryer.) That being said, it was my first professional gig and I was getting paid to be onstage.

The run of the show was mainly uneventful. Except for once

when I spilled my mango milk shake onstage in the middle of a scene, and after the performance got yelled at backstage by one of the veteran actors: *"Which one of you assholes spilled that milk shake?"*

"It was me," I said. "I'm sorry."

"You spilled a fucking milk shake in the middle of my scene!" he roared, and then just kept on yelling at me.

I apologized, but I didn't flinch, I didn't cower, and I immediately went into the assistant director's office and said, "If he talks to me that way again, ever, there will be a big problem."

One night, fifteen minutes before curtain, the actor for whom I was understudying had not shown up.

"Kunal, start warming up, you're going to have to go on," the assistant director said to me.

Woo-hoo! My moment to shine! The rest of the cast cheered me on. This is one of the wonderful things about the theater: people support each other. Even though we build walls to steel ourselves against rejection, there's something that kicks in when an actor is about to do something big and needs support. The entire cast rallied around me.

"I'm so excited for you!"

"You'll do great, Kunal!"

They were all so wonderful. I got into my costume and I warmed up for my professional acting debut.

It's time.

It wasn't time.

Just before the curtain was about to rise, the actor phoned to say that he would be there in ten minutes. He had gotten stuck on an underground train. They actually *delayed the start of the play* to give him time to get to the theater and get into costume. *My* costume. The one that I had just put on; the one that I had to take off and give back to him. My moment would have to wait.

❖

This play did, however, have one amazing perk. It was selected to represent America at the World Shakespeare Festival in Stratford-Upon-Avon, England, the birthplace of William Shakespeare. It felt so good to return to England.* For the first time in years I went to a country where I actually had a valid passport. For once, I *breezed* through immigration. I saw all of my American castmates in line and gave them the finger.

Since I didn't have shit to do in the play (I'd long since mastered the fine art of carrying a mango milk shake without spilling it), I spent most of my time geeking out in the actual Royal Shakespeare Theatre, soaking in the historic sites, and mingling with the actors from other countries. Every night, after the shows were done, performers from all over the world gathered for pints at the local pub called the Black Swan. It was amazing meeting so many artists from various walks of life. I was particularly moved by a large group of street kids from Brazil who performed *The Two Gentlemen of Verona* in Portuguese, as a musical. They had no formal training, but when I watched them perform the play it was mesmerizing. There was no fear in their performance; it came straight from the heart. No amount of training can teach you how to be in touch with what's going on inside you. They were pure love when they performed. Every night they came to the pub with their bongos and drums and basically started one big dance party. I remember watching this one beautiful Brazilian woman with dark

---

* Which is also famous as the birthplace of Kunal.

eyes, a shy smile. She wore the same dress every night because it was probably the only dress she owned. And when she danced she could make the entire world stand still.

"Kiss her," said one of the few Brazilian guys who spoke English.

"What?"

"Kiss her! In Brazilian culture, if you don't kiss the girl in the first ten minutes of meeting her, she'll think you're rude." So I mustered up the courage to make the first move, only I guess I waited a little too long, because eleven minutes later, as I prepared to walk over, she was kissing someone else.

On one of our final days in England, during a lull between performances, I relaxed in a greenroom that adjoined both the Swan Theatre and the Royal Shakespeare Theatre. It was a common room designed for actors from both theaters to have a place to eat, drink, relax, and watch TV. I sipped on a cup of coffee and watched rugby, a sport I knew very little about.

"What's the score?" asked an actor next to me, a bald guy with a booming, magical voice.

I looked up at this bald man with the beautiful voice and I did a double take. It was Sir Patrick Stewart. Patrick. Fucking. Stewart. Professor Jean-Luc X Picard was sitting next to me in the greenroom, dressed as Prospero for *The Tempest*, and he wanted to know the score.

"Ah," I said, "I'm not sure. I don't really know what's going on."

"Want me to teach you?"

"Ya-hah, pleeze?" I babbled.

So Professor X kindly explained the rules of rugby to me as we watched the game together.

Sir Patrick, if you're reading this, please do allow me to return the favor anytime with badminton.

❖

After returning from England I had to face a sober reality: my lack of any legal immigration status. If something didn't change—soon—I would be forced to head back to India. The government, as you can imagine, does not dick around when it comes to visas. The window was getting smaller every day. I had nine months left on my current student visa, and then that would be it. If I wanted to stay longer, and I did, I would need to apply for a special visa that's called the "O" visa. A visa that is described as being for "Aliens of Extraordinary Ability." No shit, that's what it's called. It makes us immigrants sound like mutants. Ha, a mutant immigrant, that's a superhero I would cheer for. Imagine: immigrant by day, superhero by night, fighting to stay illegally in America since the first Bush administration. Basically if you want to be an Alien of Extraordinary Ability, you have to give proof that the work you are doing in your field is superior to what an American can provide in the same field. Translation: An off-Broadway play wasn't going to cut it. I needed something big. I needed to do something like land a blockbuster movie or a TV show.

At that precise moment, God wasn't dropping gigs like that from the sky. Life is different when you're not in college. Suddenly you don't have the easy-to-follow road map of class, lunch, class, dinner, internship, class, school play, nookie, midterms, school play, nookie, brunch, hooky, finals, repeat three times, pick up diploma at graduation. My only real employment prospect was a low-budget play premiering in Los Angeles called *Huck & Holden*, by Rajiv Joseph. It wasn't a sitcom. It wasn't a movie. And it probably wouldn't impress the Lords of Visas. But at least it was a start. Plus I read the play and found it brilliant—it's about an Indian guy who falls in love with a black woman, and to woo this lady he has to channel Holden Caulfield from *The Catcher in the Rye*. An actor friend of mine was originally booked to star in the play, but when he had to drop out—scheduling conflicts—he suggested me for the part.

My friend talked me up to the play's director, a woman named Claudia Weill, and I decided to give her a call. I was in New York City at the time visiting cousins and figuring out my next big move. Was I going to try to stay in New York, move to Los Angeles, or go home to India? Given my visa status, these questions needed to be answered soon. I heard that Claudia was in the city, too, so I figured at least I could see her and audition. I made the call.

"I hear you're looking for an actor?"

"I'd love for you to audition."

"Great. Where should I meet you?"

"Actually, I'm not in the city right now. I'm in the Hamptons for a couple of weeks."

"Oh," I said, not knowing what the Hamptons were.

"Do you have a computer?" she asked.

"No."

"Do you have access to a computer where we can do an iChat?"

Despite my years impersonating a computer lab manager, I still wasn't that savvy with things like iChat. (This was 2006, long before FaceTime was invented.)

"No one I know has a computer with iChat," I told her honestly.

"Okay, here's an idea," Claudia said. "Why don't you go over to the Apple Store on Fifth Avenue? The new one, it looks like a huge glass box. Go there and use one of their Macs to do a quick audition for me."

What?

"Just to be clear," I said, "you want me to walk into the biggest and most crowded Apple Store in the world, stand in front of one of their computers, and use iChat to audition for your play?"

Pause.

"Sure. I think that's the best option."

"Great idea. I'm on my way there now."

I spent an hour prepping for the part, and then took the 6 train to Midtown, where, along with about two billion other people, I squeezed my way into the Apple Store.

The store was crowded as balls and I couldn't find any open Macs. It was as if all the tourists in New York had simultaneously descended upon the Apple Store to check their email. I pushed through the crowd and looked for an open spot. Nothing, nothing, nothing—*there!* I found a desktop in the corner.

I fired up iChat and called her number.

Some kid answered. It was her teenage son, who helped set up the computer.

"Hello, thanks for doing this."

"Hello?"

"HELLO?"

"Can you speak up?"

"Wait, I can't see you—"

"Is that your connection or mine?"

"HELLO?"

"KUNAL, ARE YOU THERE?"

"CLAUDIA?"

"KUNAL?"

Finally, after ten awkward minutes of scrambled connections, she could hear me and I could hear her. The store was loud and I didn't have any headphones, but what other choice did I have?

I stared at her on the screen's tiny window.

"Okay," she said, "let's see what you got."

I probably should have been nervous about the crowd of people behind me, a throng of international students who were watching me perform. But then I figured they probably didn't even speak English. Suddenly there were no tourists, no Genius Bar employees, no kids on Facebook—just me and her. I must have learned something in grad school. I delivered this emotional monologue (the climax of the play) in the middle of the store with so much passion that I began to cry. I finished the monologue and wiped my tears.

Another pause.

"I want you to come to Los Angeles and play this character for me." Before I could respond she continued, "I can only pay you seven dollars per show, and there will only be thirty people in the audience at every performance. But I can tell you that a lot of people in the industry will be watching."

Hmmmm. I mean, I did like the play. A lot. But this would require moving across the country for . . . seven dollars per show? You make more than that at Taco Bell, and there at least you get free chalupas.

"Can I think about it?"

"Sure. Let me know first thing tomorrow morning."

Dazed, I pushed through the ocean of people and I left the Apple Store. There was only one person who I needed to speak to right now. It was 2 a.m. in New Delhi but I called him immediately. *C'mon, pick up, pick up, pick up . . .*

"Are you okay?" my father asked.

It was a reasonable question, as you normally never call someone at 2 a.m. unless you're 1) not okay or 2) drunk and you want to sleep with them. Neither was the case right then.

"I'm fine, Dad. I was just offered this chance to be in a play in Los Angeles."

I told him all the details, especially the part about how it paid only seven dollars, would only have an audience of thirty people per show, and how it clearly wasn't an important enough performance to impress the Gods of the Visa Office.

Without hesitating my father asked, "Do you have any other offers?"

"Huh?"

"Is anyone else offering you a chance to work?"

"No."

"Then go."

"It's that simple?" I asked.

"Kunal, what's the point of weighing the pros and cons if you only have one option? There's nothing to think about. Move to Los Angeles."

Classic Dad. He always had—and continues to have—the best perspective. So often in life we agonize, we deliberate, and we beat ourselves up to carefully evaluate the reasons we should or should not do something. But usually it's so much simpler. *If you have no other offers, take the one offer you have.* He wasn't concerned about the money. I had been living off my earnings from working in Washington, D.C., and Stratford, but they were wearing thin. He told me that if I needed money in LA, I could just get a job there. That's what people do. They pick up the pieces of what they have and move on. Civilizations were built on this very principle.

My parents had set up a support system for me where I couldn't fail. Success wasn't defined by income or status or becoming famous. That wasn't important to them. What was important to them was my happiness. They've always told me that if things don't work out for me in America, I will always have a home to come back to. What was important to them was me not turning into an asshole. Sometimes people say, "Wow, *Big Bang Theory*—your parents must be proud of you." I like to think that they were proud of me before *Big Bang*. They don't care that I'm an actor. They just care that I'm their kid. And a happy one at that.

The next morning I accepted the job.

I was on my way to LA.

The Waiting Period (Extended Mix)

HUCK AND HOLDEN WAS BEING STAGED IN A THEATER IN EAST LA. If you know anything about LA geography, you will laugh at my decision to stay at an apartment in Santa Monica. Even though it is only twenty miles away, at seven dollars a show, my broke ass couldn't afford a car, so every day I spent four hours on the public bus system. I shared a one-bedroom apartment with this very sweet albeit manic-depressive girl. I was sleeping on the couch but paying half the rent, which in hindsight may not have been fair.

During one scene in *Huck and Holden*, a library of about five hundred books crashes to the ground, which meant that every night after the play, an intern at the theater would spend two hours cleaning up the books and arranging them in neat little stacks. I didn't have any friends yet and I was desperate for company, so, after each performance, instead of going home to my lonely couch, I stayed at the theater and helped stack the books.

"Kunal, you don't have to do that," said Claudia, the director.

"Oh, I'm happy to help," I told her, not admitting that I simply had nowhere else to go.

Claudia was a lady of her word: It was true that the production only had thirty audience members each night. But it was also true, as she had promised, that the crowd was full of industry na-bobs. On opening night, the curtain went up and I could see Mi-chael Lynton, the president of Sony Pictures, in the audience. (I had heard he was coming and googled his picture.) He was sitting next to John Lithgow. And there was Tony Shalhoub. And Denzel Washington. *Holy shit, she's the real deal.*

The play was a success. But I needed to make some real money to survive in LA. I combed Craigslist for jobs and I came across a listing for Gerardo's Raw, a raw food restaurant. They were look-ing for waiters. Most actors in LA wait tables, because it allows them to make cash at night while leaving their days open for au-ditions. Since I'd never really had experience waiting tables, I was surprised when I got a call to interview for the open position. I had no clue what raw food was, but I showed up for the interview with a big smile on my face nevertheless.

"Do you like raw food?" the owner asked.

"I love it," I said. "Raw means you cook it without oil?"

"No. It means there's no cooking. At all."

"Um. Yeah. That's what I meant. No oil. No nothing . . ."

For reasons known only to them, they hired me to wait tables on Monday, Tuesday, and Wednesday nights. (I couldn't work the rest of the nights because of the play.) Suddenly I was around peo-ple again and soon I felt right at home. I befriended the owner, Ge-rardo, who hung around all day wearing tiny shorts and no shirt.*
I became particularly close to Diego, an energetic guy who had the whitest teeth of any man I had ever seen. I marveled at his zest for life. He had two jobs: he woke up at five in the morning to cook breakfast burritos for a beachside shack, then he cooked

---

* It was a little weird seeing so much skin, even in a raw food restaurant.

fish tacos there for lunch, and then, at 4 p.m., he came to Gerardo's for the dinner shift, where he made raw cacao milk shakes and chopped all the vegetables for the salads. Seven days a week, 365 days a year, two jobs, four shifts, not one complaint.

Diego took a lot of pride in his work. "Come eat my fish tacos," he told me one day. I could tell it meant a lot to him, so I decided to join him on the pier at his little beach shack. It overlooked the ocean, and we each sat with a fish taco in our hand wrapped in tinfoil. We cracked open a couple of Coronas.

"Eat," he said, eagerly awaiting my approval.

I took a bite. I closed my eyes. I felt the crunch of the breaded fish, the spice of the salsa, lime, cilantro, sour cream, a hint of jalapeño. "Diego, best fish taco ever."

That was music to his ears. He released a loud laugh, his head tilting to the sky. "I toldju, mang!" And he began to devour his own fish taco, shredding it, making these loud lip-smacking noises. I had the impression he was enjoying his taco much more today because he got to share it with someone.

I reached for my Corona as the sun was just getting ready to go to sleep.

I washed down my taco and looked over at Diego. He was quiet. Enjoying the sunset.

"I have to go to work," he said as he got up to go.

That was it. That was his moment of elation. A fish taco, a friend, a beer, and a sunset.

❖

Every night a guy came in who looked like he had just walked out of a WWF ring. He always wore a suit with a turtleneck instead of a shirt, rocked sunglasses indoors, and had long blond hair that someone later told me was a wig. Zane. What a guy. He always came in alone and sat at a corner table, scribbling in his notebook. "Is Diego here?" he'd ask every night. "Can you ask him to make my milk shake Diego-thick?" (Diego made the thickest chocolate milk shakes. This became a running joke between us: "His milk shakes bring all the boys to the yard.")

Zane drove to the restaurant in the most insanely beautiful cars; it seemed like a different one each time: Ferrari, Jaguar, Porsche, you name it. But my personal favorite was a yellow Lamborghini. Ever since I was a kid in New Delhi, I've associated real success with driving a yellow Lamborghini. When you're a little kid you measure success by the accumulation of big, shiny toys, whereas when you're an adult, you learn the real measure of success: the accumulation of big, shiny toys.

❖

The buzz from *Huck and Holden* had begun to spread. It helped open doors for me. I only had nine months left on my student visa and I knew it was imperative that I get an agent. Claudia had helped me get a few meetings with some of the bigger agencies, even though I didn't have many TV credits under my belt.* A lot of them said no, they couldn't represent me, because they were worried about my visa; in nine months, I could be sent back to India.

No, no, no, no.

And then, suddenly, out of the blue, *not* no.

Thursday: Met with a smaller agency. Clicked with an agent named Suzanne right away. She liked me and I liked her.

---

* Okay, I'd had one scene on *NCIS* playing an Iranian terrorist with a crooked mustache. Indian. Iranian. We all look the same.

Friday, 11 a.m.: I was called in to sign papers with this agency.

Friday, 1 p.m.: Suzanne, my new agent for all of 120 minutes, called to say, "Kunal, we've got you an audition for a new pilot. It's for a new Chuck Lorre show."

"Oh, that sounds great," I said, not really knowing who Chuck Lorre was.

"The audition is on Monday," she said. "I'll send you the sides; you'll have the weekend to prepare."

"I'm going to book it for you," I told her, smiling.

I'm going to book it for you.

We both laughed—who the hell did I think I was?

I didn't *really* have confidence that I would book the role, because frankly, I didn't even fully understand what was happening. I was just delighted to have an actual agent send me on an actual audition for an actual TV show. This lack of experience helped me. I was loose. I didn't know enough to grasp the importance of the moment and get nervous.

When I got the script for *Big Bang*, I read it and instantly loved it. For all the reasons lots of viewers love the show, I love it, too. Sharp writing. Engaging characters. The part they wanted me to audition for was, of course, a character named "David." Yep, Raj was originally named David Koothrappali, and even though his last name sounded Indian, they were not looking for any specific ethnicity. I mean, when I walked into the audition it literally looked like a lineup for the new United Colors of Benetton campaign.

I had the weekend to prepare for this audition, and I went deep into my bag of acting tools. I broke down the character of David; I dissected him from every angle. Let's start with the accent. In the script he could have been from anywhere, but I knew that a lot of my strength lay in the cadence of my dialect, so I decided to make him from India proper, and not just *from* India, but fresh off the boat. I imagined what my New Delhi accent would sound like if I were only a year or two removed from India—maybe how I'd sounded as a freshman in college.

I researched David's signature personality trait, selective mutism, and read up on the underlying psychology. I learned that selective mutism is a disease that stems from pathological shyness. It is a real thing. So, what renders someone speechless? It's not that Dave is dumbfounded. He's *trying* to speak. The research says that your brain is sending a signal to your mouth, but somewhere along the way, you emotionally block your mouth from making words. And I thought, *Okay, what would make me, Kunal, selectively mute?* I imagined meeting one of my idols, such as the legendary cricket demigod Sachin Tendulkar. If Sachin happened to turn up one night when I was working at the raw food restaurant, what would that physically do to me? I knew that my mouth would open and my mind would have a thousand things to say but nothing would come out. I would probably tense my shoulders and my jaw, tighten my butt cheeks, dart my eyes back and forth to avoid contact, and try to become as small as possible, like a tortoise who doesn't have a shell. And what if Sachin was *always* around me? Well, that would be Dave with selective mutism.

On Monday, instead of taking the bus, I treated myself to a thirteen-dollars-a-day rental car, and I left so early for the audition—three hours early—that I drove forty miles in the wrong direction, called Suzanne, had to make a U-turn, and I *still* made it there on time. (Kids, if you ever want anything in life, always be early to meetings.)

The preliminary audition was at 11 a.m. I wore brown corduroy pants, a checkered shirt buttoned to the top, and a Caltech hat. (In the pilot, if you remember, Raj is wearing a hat.) Here's how the process works: At the preliminary audition, you perform for the casting director, who in turn either dismisses you or gives you "acting notes"—things they'd like to see you do differently for the second round. The second round (if you make it) is where you get to audition for the actual producers. During the first round, though, the casting director's notes typically involve your delivery and motivation—you know—acting shit.

"Kunal, can you unbutton the top button of your shirt?" she asked.

"Sure, no problem."

And those were my notes. A few minutes later the casting director took two of us aside. "Can you guys come back at three p.m. for round two?" She sent everyone else home, which, frankly, is an actor's *dream*—to have almost every other competitor sent home after the first round.

I had a few hours to kill and I was feeling confident, so I went outside and ate a bacon cheeseburger (so of course I thought of Allison the Lesbian). I wore a napkin over my shirt, terrified that I would destroy my costume.

I came back at two thirty—thirty minutes early—and was the first person back. As I sat in the hallway the casting director and the producers walked past me and I made a silly joke, something like, "I had a cheeseburger for lunch so please excuse my gas."

This made everyone crack up. I was trying to win them over even before my audition.

"You are so funny!" the casting director said as she went into the room.

Yes, I'm funny! When you're an actor you hold on to every single word from a casting director, and you analyze and overanalyze everything they say—over and over and over again until you get the part, or more likely, you don't.

I was called into the room and it was time to audition for Chuck Lorre and Bill Prady, the creators of *The Big Bang Theory*. The truth is I still did not understand the gravitas of the situation. A more seasoned actor might have been psyching themselves out: *Oh God, it's Chuck Lorre! He's created like six of the biggest sitcoms of all time! He's a god in the television world! This is my big chance, don't screw it up!* To me, he was just another guy I wanted to make laugh.

Chuck has a maniacal laugh, a cackle that's almost a cough. It's infectious to hear that laugh. It's a laugh that makes you want to laugh along with it. So when he started laughing at my audition it gave me more and more confidence and I began to take over the room. It was another *sssssssssss* moment, but this time it was real life.

I could tell that the audition had gone well. I went home, showered, and headed to my usual shift at the raw food restaurant, waiting tables and bullshitting with Diego and Zane. The next day once again I went to work for my usual shift . . . and then saw I had four missed calls.

"Kunal, they want to screen-test you," said Suzanne.

"What?"

"They want to test you. Tomorrow."

In the pilot world, a screen test is the final step to securing the role. To play Dave, I would have to audition for the big cheeses at Warner Bros. and CBS.

I finished my shift at the restaurant—at least I think I did. I don't remember anything else about that evening, I was walking around in a daze. That night I couldn't sleep. Both excited and nervous. *This was real.*

The next morning, once again, I treated myself to a rental car from Enterprise. This was a big moment, and I didn't want to take my chances on the public transportation system. They happened to be out of economy cars that day, so instead they upgraded me, for free, to a white convertible Toyota Solara. What a good start to the day! On the way I opened the roof and blasted nineties hip-hop, feeling the wind in my hair and the California sun on my face. It was Broadway, and Central Park, and daydreaming all over again. I drove through the gate at CBS Studios feeling like a champ.

The final audition was in a "black box" type of theater. It looked exactly like all the theaters I had auditioned in before, and so it felt oddly comfortable. This was auditioning for ACTF. This was auditioning for grad school. *I have been here before.*

I stood on that stage and knew that the most powerful people in the studio were watching me, so I decided I would break the ice with a stupid joke.

"Hello, I am Kunal. Thank you for allowing me to audition for *Two and a Half Men.*"

Laughter from the faceless audience.

"No, wait, that's not right," I continued. "What Chuck Lorre show is this? Just too many to choose from."

Before I started, I said to the casting director, in front of the entire audience, "Listen, I'm saying these lines in a room full of *very important people*, so it's important to me that you don't crack up laughing in the middle of my audition. Please keep it together."

She starts laughing and the faceless audience does, too.

At that moment I'm just at a party, telling jokes to my friends, entertaining the room.

Then I deliver my audition. More laughter, and some more, and maybe a little more . . .

After it was over, driving back to Enterprise in that white convertible, I said to myself, *Kunal, no matter what happened, you did a really good job, you left your heart on the line, and I'm proud of you. Even if you don't get the job, I'm proud of you.*

❖

And then the phone didn't ring.

It didn't ring that night.

It didn't ring the next day.

It didn't ring the third day.

It didn't ring the fourth day.

Typically, the way this whole thing works is that you find out if you get the role within five days of an audition. This is contractually required. On day five, if the studio needs more time, they have to officially ask your agent if they can "extend the waiting period."

So on day five—the day that I should get a yes or no—they asked to extend the waiting period.

I had no leverage. After huddling with my manager and agent, we agreed to extend the waiting period for another five days.

No call on day six.

No call on day seven.

Nor on day eight.

And not on day nine.

I'm hapless, I'm sleepless, I'm waiting, I'm hanging on by a thread. Hoping for a miracle. Bewitched, bothered, and bewildered. You get the picture.

Finally, on day ten, I got the long-awaited call from my agent.

But it wasn't that call.

"Kunal, they want to extend another five days."

Kill me. But what could I do? At that point I had become a zombie. I was still working at the raw food restaurant, but I couldn't focus on the food or Diego or Zane or Zane's yellow Lamborghini. I would take the bus to work, arrive for my shift, and not even remember how I got there.

We agreed to extend another five days—what choice did we have?

No call on day eleven.

No call on day twelve.

No call on day thirteen.

No call on day fourteen.

Finally, on day fifteen, I got the call from my agent.

But it was not that call.

"They want to extend for another five days."

"No," I said. I had had enough. "I demand an answer. This is torture."

"Kunal. We have to."

"If they give me the role they give me the role, but if not, I'm out."

"*Trust me*," my agent said.

"No. No more." I was adamant.

"Okay, how about this. I'll tell them that we can extend the waiting period *one last time*, five more days, and that's it."

I let out a long, deep sigh.

"One last time," I agreed.

No call on day sixteen.

No calls on days seventeen, eighteen, or nineteen.

And still nothing on day twenty.

It was time to call the studio and tell them that we would not extend anymore.

"Give us a couple more hours, and we'll call you back," the studio promised her.

Then, finally, I got the call.

It was that call.

I was going to play Dave on *The Big Bang Theory*. Only now he was going to be called Raj Koothrappali.

It's funny how it all worked out. The beginning was quick as lightning—I auditioned for an agent on Thursday, signed with the agent on Friday, auditioned for *Big Bang* on Monday, had a callback on Wednesday—and then, toward the end, it all came to a soul-crushing halt. One thing I learned, though, is that whenever you go into auditions or interviews, *the judge is on your side.* They want you to succeed. Think about it. Let's say you're going to interview for a job. The hiring manager wants to fill that job so she can recruit a kick-ass employee and grow her team. And she wants that employee to be you. She's hoping that you'll blow her mind. As actors, or as job seekers, we walk into the room and we worry that they're sniffing for weakness. The truth is that they're already on your side, because once they find someone they want, they can call it a day and go home.

Luck. People always say to me. *You got lucky with your first audition.* What do I say to them? How can I explain the journey? Leaving everyone and everything I knew in Delhi, cleaning toilets in Portland, making it through graduate school in Philadelphia, spilling milk shakes in D.C., auditioning in the Apple Store in New York City, stacking books every night, and riding the bus across LA. All the heartache, all those years, all the winning and losing and winning again. Every person has a different journey. But no one has an easy one. *Luck.*

❖

After I received the good news I still had a few shifts to finish at Gerardo's. I informed everyone that I would soon be leaving.

On my final night at the restaurant, Zane came in wearing his usual suit and his usual sunglasses. "I have a present for you," he said, tossing me a box.

I opened it. Inside was a miniature yellow Lamborghini. On the bottom of the box he wrote, "Till you get your own."

James Bond and the Mouse

ONE OF MY FATHER'S FANTASIES IS THAT HE IS AN INTERNA-
tional superspy who specializes in outdoor survival. He has never
openly confessed this to me, but his actions scream "superspy plus
mountain man survivalist."

For example, every time he comes to Los Angeles to visit, his
first request is to shop at an outdoors store. This trip, which re-
quires a three-hour drive to the suburbs, ends up being a whole-
day affair. We wake up early enough to have some tea and biscuits
and to drop my mother off at Target* and we set off to the wilder-
ness that is the suburbs. Along the way I can feel the excitement
building in my father. It is the same excitement he probably sensed
in me as a child when he took me to the toy store, or for ice cream,
or to play badminton.

It gives me immense pride to be able to do this for my father.
After a lifetime of being taken care of, it really is nice to be the one
taking care. Halfway through the drive, he is asleep. I, too, am trying to stay awake. I blast some Bollywood hits and focus hard on
the road ahead. My mind is drifting, and with every floating leaf,

---

* An expedition that deserves an entire book in itself.

every passing cloud, I reminisce about my father, about this man asleep by my side, the man who shaped my very being, and his childlike enthusiasm for our trip to the outdoors store.

❖

My father always collected guns. We grew up in a household with guns. When I was seven I was called into the gun room and taught how to clean guns. As I got older I was taught gun safety. How to load and unload a gun and, most important, how to make sure the safety catch was always on. The gun room smelled like gunpowder and oil. It was a room with thick steel cabinets. It felt like a bank vault. And it was cold, always cold. But it felt secure. Like if shit went down, this gun room would protect us. It had a personality of its own. It was RoboCop.

One day when I was ten my mother had to go out of town for some work. When Mom was out of town, my brother and I would sleep in my parents' room on the floor. This was mainly to cut down on the cost of running two ACs in the house. The summers in New Delhi were so hot that we needed to run the AC twenty-four hours a day. Obviously all of our neighbors were also doing the same thing, which would lead the electricity circuit breaker for our area to overheat and basically blow up. This meant that depending on what street you lived on, you would lose power for three hours a day between certain hours in order to protect the breaker. Our street was selected for 10 p.m. to 1 a.m., the exact hours when we would be trying to go to sleep. Already hot and bothered, Dad was in a real huff on this particular night. We were on the floor in his room, wiggling around, frustrated by the sauna in which we were stuffed, waiting for the AC to come back to life.

I heard my father tossing and turning, occasionally releasing an audible expletive. I've always been a light sleeper, and I could tell that he was getting more and more agitated. His expletives were getting louder and he seemed to be really angry.

"Goddammit, I've had enough," he said, and suddenly ripped himself out of bed.

I jumped out of bed, too. "Papa, what happened?"

"*Beta* [son], there is a stupid mouse running up and down and he just got on the bed and ran all over my face! I'm going to kill that asshole once and for all. Go get my rifle."

He threw me the keys to the gun room, and a rush of excitement ran over me. I always relished a meeting with RoboCop. I was surprised he asked me and not my older brother, but I quickly realized it was because my brother was asleep and snoring. Fat-ass. I ran to the gun room, opened the door, and took a deep breath as the odor of gun oil and gunpowder filled my lungs. I felt alive, like a raging bull. I was ten, high on some mix of toxins, I had a rifle in my hand, and I was about to watch the massacre of a mouse. Best. Night. Ever. Upon returning to the bedroom, I found my brother was awake and shining a flashlight under the bed.

"Is the safety on?" Dad asked.

"Yes, Papa."

"Good boy, now stand behind your brother. Keep an eye on the mouse; when I shoot it you have to keep track of the splattered blood."

YYYYEEEEEESSSS, I heard in my head. I was swimming with adrenaline. Dad effortlessly cocked the gun and took aim. There was silence. Everything suddenly went still. My brother was calm as a horse, steady hands as he held that flashlight directly at the mouse. He's always been a rock under pressure, I envy him for that. THWACK! THWACK! THWACK! Three shots rang out.*

"Did you see the blood, Kunal?"

"No, Dad, I didn't see anything."

"Can you boys see the mouse?"

"No, Dad," we replied.

There was no blood. There was no mouse. We damn near turned that entire bed upside down to find the remains of that mouse. But nothing. Not even a blemish of blood on the wall. I mean, three bullet holes in the wall, sure, but a dead mouse? Nope. Where could it have gone? Had this little mouse outplayed the massive aliens with guns and lived to see another day? Was it all a figment of our imagination? Had the heat driven us mad? No one could figure it out.

What we did know is that there was one bullet left in the magazine. Now, Dad didn't want to leave a loaded rifle in the house, and we could not unload it because it was already in the slot. The only other option was to shoot out the remaining bullet. So Dad took the gun into the bathroom and shot into the clothes basket. Not a bucket of water, or into some foam, or the sky, but into a pile of dirty laundry.

When Mom came home the next day she had a lot of questions. We mainly hid from her, and when she asked us why there were bullet holes in all her clothes we played dumb and said things like "Hungry moths, probably." We never told her the truth. Maybe my father confessed. He was never one to stare death in the eye, and telling the truth was much easier than facing Medusa's wrath.

_____

* In case you're worried, there was no real danger of the bullets going through the thick cement walls or the hard marble floors and injuring anyone.

Maybe when she reads this book it will suddenly all make sense. I sometimes wonder what happened to that mouse. I imagine him sitting on the beach somewhere, in a hula skirt, smoking a cigar, drinking a Corona, reminiscing like me.

❖

Dad has just woken up. We are close and he can probably smell the outdoors store from three miles away. A sense of smell is a wonderful thing to have. Every shop has a smell. Especially the ones we love. Toys "R" Us always smells like flowers and plastic, McDonald's always smells like french fries, and outdoors stores always smell like freedom. I never asked Dad what outdoors stores smelled like, but I'm pretty sure that's the way they smelled to him. We walk into the mega-complex of everything outdoorsy and are completely overcome by the sheer size of this place. Though we have been here before, it always feels like we're arriving for the first time.

When I was growing up in India we didn't have anything like "superstores." Everything was mom-and-pop owned. Sure, things are changing now, we have huge malls and such, but for someone from anywhere outside America to walk into a place like this is jaw-dropping. America does truly grasp the concept of overabundance. We grab a shopping cart and begin to head down the aisles one by one. Dad is giddy. He is going through all the aisles with an air of pride about mankind. He is proud of the designs and the research and labor that have gone into creating these products that help us brave the elements.

He grabs a headlamp and tries it on. He's always buying headlamps. I don't understand why. We make fun of him for it and he's oddly quiet when we do. Maybe he really does use them. Maybe when there is load shedding on our street he secretly goes out and helps all the neighbors turn on their generators. Maybe he is "Super Headlamp Man," protector of all when darkness falls over the neighborhood.

We continue through the metropolis, lamp still on his head, when we land at the outerwear section. This, to my father, is Mecca. My father worked in the garment trade at one point, and he is always in awe of the linings to be found in high-tech outerwear. It's never cold enough in New Delhi to wear any of these things, but still he's touching all of them, letting out oohs and aahs with every caress of stitching. He begins to pull them off the rack and try them on, inspecting every pocket as he does. Just a tip: the more pockets the better. I think I once bought him a jacket with forty-seven pockets. Really.

And then, we see it. The mother lode of jackets! The one that is so big it takes two mannequins to hold up. The one that you can wear in the Arctic Circle, the one that can swallow you whole. Dad tries it on, of course, and his head instantly disappears. I can hear a muffled voice inspecting the inside seams of this masterpiece, this master beast. I can hear him say something about sweating or blacking out or something, and I realize that he is asking me to help get it off him. I manage to get him out of it and we put it back on the mannequin. I think Dad has met his match. That just may be too much jacket for one man, or even two men. As we continue on toward the end of our shopping spree, I take account of the stockpile in the shopping cart. Headlamps, insect repellent (extra strength, obviously, for India), a light Windbreaker that can fold into a small sock, a police baton (why? I don't ask), a few key chain torches, and a bottle of Diet Coke.

As we check out, my father begins to chat with the checkout

lady. He is the king of small talk. Within two minutes we learned that this lady is from Guatemala and her parents came to America when she was a child, and her parents have since gone back to retire. She has two children, both in college, and her husband is the manager of the store. On the way out she invites us over for dinner if we're ever back in the area.

After we load the car full of our goodies, I say to Dad, "Is there anything else you'd like to get, just on the off chance we *never* come back to the outdoors store again?"

He thinks. And he thinks some more.

I know what he's thinking. He is negotiating price points and pondering the logistics of carrying a twenty-pound arctic jacket back home in his luggage. I know he wants to buy it, but he would never use it. We all have things like that.

"No. I'm tired, Kunal. Let's go home."

I excuse myself and say I have to use the restroom. I run back to the store, holler at my new Guatemalan lady friend, and disappear into the aisles. Fifteen minutes later with the help of the store manager I carry out what looks like the carcass of the Abominable Snowman. I make it over to the car and see Dad beaming from ear to ear. He knew what I was up to, I knew that he knew, and the store manager, who didn't know, now knew.

On the way home Dad falls asleep again. I, on the other hand, am not tired. I think about my mom. It's been almost seven hours since we dropped her off at Target and she hasn't even called once.

Always Joy

Inside me lives a little boy.

He is the little boy who smiles at strangers.

The little boy who wakes up wanting to play.

The little boy who wants no harm to come to any man.

The little boy who is unwavering in his hope.

The little boy who sleeps in comfort.

The little boy who eats and drinks what *he wants,*

When *he wants.*

He wishes all the wars in the world would end.

And that there was no pain.

And no man would die.

He is a shy little boy.

But sometimes he feels not so little and not so shy.

Sometimes he feels like a tiger.

He is the same little boy who is afraid of the dark.

And of monsters, and bears, and spiders.

He is afraid of people wanting to do bad things to him.

He makes up stories in his head.

All the time.

He is playing and fighting invisible foes.

He is growing and spinning and trying and failing.

He feels not so much like a little boy.

He wants to be a man.

He wants to flex his muscles and intimidate the weak.

He wants to protect his woman and take on the world.

He wants to make money

And be famous

And make more money

And be handsome

And have many

Cars

And

Lovers

And

Houses

And

Maybe

A plane.

Just one.

One day he would like a little boy of his own.

A boy he creates with his woman.

So he can tell his own little boy

That

The little boy will always have

A little boy inside him, too.

And that little boy

Will always be afraid of the dark

And of monsters and bears and lions.

Someday he will grow,

But

A part of him

Will always just

Be

A little boy.

Just

Like

Him.

K. N.
April 2, 2012
Laurel Canyon
Los Angeles, CA

Thirteen Things I've Learned from Playing an Astrophysicist on TV

1. I AM NOT AN ASTROPHYSICIST.

Sometimes fans of the show will approach me and they'll want me to be smart. It's always awkward when I let them down gently and explain that, in fact, I am only an actor who is playing an astrophysicist. This just crushes some people. They want me to *be* Raj. One guy asked me, "Hey, what do you think about the Higgs boson particle? Now we can finally prove that dark matter exists!"

"I'm sorry, I don't speak English very well, but I'm with you," I said.

The only smart thing I know is that eight glasses of water a day is too much water.

2. I'M AN ADDICT.

Mints. I am addicted to mints. When you're doing scenes with fellow actors and speaking into their face, ideally, you don't want your breath to smell like fish. So, to compensate for my fear of bad breath, I think I have consumed about three and a half million Altoids on the set of *Big Bang*.

Actually, I can do the math:

On average I consume 2 Altoids an hour.

Each workday is 10 hours.

Each week we have 5 workdays.

Every episode takes 1 week to film.

Every season has 24 episodes.

We have done 8 seasons.

2 x 10 x 5 x 1 x 24 x 8 = 19,200 Altoids

3. WE'RE ALL OBSESSED WITH PING-PONG.

It's not a secret that everyone in the *Big Bang* cast is a Ping-Pong fanatic. We have three tables on set and the games are ferociously competitive. Kaley Cuoco-Sweeting is a very good Ping-Pong player. Mark Cendrowski, our director, is excellent. And I *think* I'm the best. Kaley plays like a jackhammer, smashing the ball back at you. (She's just like Addy, my old badminton rival, except way hotter.) My style is more smooth and silky—more finessey.

We staged tournaments on set that became so intense, so competitive, that we literally had to shut the operation down last year. People were getting injured. Someone dove for a ball and tore their ACL, one of the guys ran into a ladder and needed rotator cuff surgery, we had a lot of cuts and bruises, and once I sprained my ankle. We even started challenging other TV shows; we took on Kelsey Grammer's sitcom *Back to You*. I would tell you who won but I am sworn to secrecy.*

---

* We won.

4. IT'S NOT A LAUGH TRACK.

I constantly hear people say, "I like that show, but it needs to stop using a laugh track." Now hear this: WE DON'T USE A LAUGH TRACK. The laughter is real, from a real live audience. I know this because I am there every single day of my life. In the same way that theater actors, stand-up comedians, and musicians perform in front of a live audience, that's how we do it. And we love it because it gives us instant feedback.

On the contrary, we do have to occasionally *remove* laughter from the audio track, as the most devoted fans in the live audience, at times, know the characters so well that they anticipate the joke and giggle before it happens. When this happens, we off them. Just kidding. We give them a warning and if they do it again, *then* we off them. Really, we love our fans and it's such a blessing to see so many people connect with the show. We don't take this for granted.

5. SELECTIVE MUTISM IS A REAL THING.

Before I played Raj, I had no idea that there really is such a thing as pathological shyness. It's a diagnosed psychological condition, and yes, it really can lead to selective mutism, the reason for Raj's inability to speak to women. I've received heartwarming letters from parents of children suffering from the condition, and who said, "Thank you for being the voice of selective mutism." (And the irony of that statement was not lost on me.)

For me, the real problem with my character having selective mutism on *The Big Bang Theory* is that it has meant that Raj has to drink so much alcohol. When I drink those grasshopper "martinis," they're actually made from water, cream, and a heavy splash of green food coloring. After a tape night, I literally poop green for, like, three days.

6. I'M A FANBOY AT HEART.

I'm as big a fan of the show as anybody you'll ever meet. I love *Big Bang*. I love playing Raj. Each week, we get the new script on Tuesday night after we finish taping. Whenever I get a new script, I can't wait to tear it open and see what our writers have in store for us. Every Tuesday night feels like Christmas morning.

7. THE CAMERA REALLY DOES ADD TWENTY POUNDS.

And then craft services adds another thirty. The truth is that when you're on set, there's unlimited food at your disposal, always, everywhere. Nothing but M&Ms and chocolate bars and cookies and cake, because the entire industry runs on sugar and carbs and Coca-Cola.

8. NO ONE'S A CELEBRITY WHEN WAITING FOR A CAR.

Here's how the Emmys, SAG Awards, and Golden Globes really work: We all get dressed up and apply makeup and stand sweating on the red carpet, and a few hours later, the 99 percent of us who don't go home as winners are so miserable that we drink ourselves into a stupor, and then, several more hours later, when the party is over we all go outside and wait in the valet line for our limos. It's always a chaotic forty-five-minute wait, with parking attendants using bullhorns to call out limo numbers. We're all just sitting, sometimes lying down on the pavement, waiting for our cars. Even the award-winning actors are rubbing their feet, tired and cranky, holding their statues in one hand, iPhones in the other, trying to pull as many strings as they can to get their car ahead in the limo line. *"You said five minutes twenty minutes ago!"* We are all equals in that moment. The biggest stars look like the most petty kids, cutting in line, pushing each other out of the way, screaming at parking attendants. It's like a riot with the most beautifully dressed protestors in the world.

9. YOU DON'T NEED TO GO BIG FOR THE LAUGH.

This has taken me some time to learn. Given my theater background, I was used to playing things BIG. You can't go small in theater. You have to really physicalize every emotion, because the guy in the twenty-fifth row simply can't see a subtle twitching of your lip. On TV? You're practically zoomed into the actor's nostrils. It took me a few years—maybe until season four, if I'm being totally honest—to stop forcing it. You don't need to sell the joke. When the writing is as good as ours, just trust it; just say the words and the joke will sell itself.

10. MY IDOLS DIDN'T DISAPPOINT.

You always hear about someone meeting their idol . . . and then discovering they're not how they'd imagined them to be. It's like how I felt when I met Stephen Hawking: total prick. KIDDING. Actually, he's the best example of the point I'm trying to make. On *Big Bang*, I've been lucky to meet so many of my idols—Stan

Lee, James Earl Jones, Leonard Nimoy, George Takei, Stephen Hawking, so many others—and they've been lovely and charming and wonderful. But the cool thing is that I've seen them as *human beings*, and rather than knock them off their pedestal, that just makes them even more amazing. We sit side by side in the makeup room and make small talk about this and that, and you realize that we are all just working. They're working, and you're working, and like all human beings, we just show up to work and we do our jobs.

When I met Stephen Hawking I knew that I was in the presence of a great man, and I felt bad, at first, that Howard was doing a Stephen Hawking impression *right in front of him.* Were we being dicks? I thought maybe, but then I saw that Dr. Hawking was smiling, and later I heard that he enjoyed the rehearsal so much, in fact, that he went back home and reread the script. I've also heard that Stephen Hawking likes to party with strippers, but I didn't bring that up with him.

11. YOU DON'T BREAK A COMEDIAN'S FLOW WHEN THEY'RE WORKING.

One of Raj's idiosyncrasies is that he has selective mutism, so in scenes during a taping, I'll whisper into the ears of the male characters, who then, in turn, vocalize my thoughts to women. Do I mess with the other actors when I'm whispering, trying to crack them up?

The truth is that I don't. We always say that we're very serious about our funny. The language on our show is very specific, almost like a poem, and we don't do any ad-libbing at all. If you mess with someone you can break his or her rhythm. That said, I'm the absolute worst on the show about breaking character and cracking up laughing. I'll even start laughing at my own jokes, even before I get to the punch li—Bwahaha. Hooohaha. HAHAHA!

Yeah, I'm even annoying myself right now.

12. TV FAME IS DIFFERENT FROM MOVIE FAME.

This is not to say that I'm "famous." I'm not. Or maybe I am. I don't care either way. Let's just say I'm *popular*. But when I started to get noticed after season three—the year we went into syndication—I realized that, as a TV personality, because I am in someone's living room each and every night, people feel like they already know me.

When a show plays in a family's living room several times a week, it's part of family time between parents and kids and cousins and grandparents. It's a familiar thing that's almost part of your house, like a couch or a jar of mayonnaise in the back of the fridge. So when people see me walking on the street, they feel like we're old pals. Women pull my cheeks and men clap me on the shoulder; I'm like a little petting zoo. But *movie stars*, on the other hand, are much more *untouchable*. Those are people that you watch from afar. They're regal lions. I'm a friendly goat.

13. . . . AND I LIKE IT.

Obviously I'm supposed to say something humble like, "Aw, shucks, I'm just happy to do my job, and I don't even pay attention to things like getting recognized in public, or being asked to sign autographs, or having lots of Twitter followers. None of that matters compared to the Work." The truth is that all of that is incredibly fun. Anyone who says otherwise is either a liar or a Cylon.

I enjoy that stuff because:

1. It's an appreciation of my work. As a professional actor, this gives me pride. I'm happy when my work makes others happy.

2. I recognize that this might be fleeting. Who knows where my career will take me. Maybe people won't recognize me anymore when *Big Bang* ends. Maybe there's a career lull. Maybe I'll be hit by a bus or die of an Altoids overdose or be sent to prison, finally convicted for the time that I ▮▮▮▮▮▮ ▮▮▮▮▮▮▮▮▮▮▮▮▮▮▮▮▮▮▮▮▮▮▮▮▮▮▮▮▮▮▮▮▮▮ ▮▮▮▮▮▮▮▮▮▮▮▮▮▮ We never know where life will take us. So I'm trying to follow my father's advice and enjoy the life I have, and to love with a big heart.

A Thought Recorded on an Aeroplane Cocktail Napkin

EATING SHITTY IS LIKE A ONE-NIGHT STAND. INSTANT GRATIFICATION FOLLOWED BY A LOT OF QUESTIONS.

And Then I Fell in Love

"SHE'S AN EX–MISS INDIA. YOU NEED TO MEET HER," SAID MY
cousin.

"Ex? Can't you introduce me to the current one?" I joked.

The woman in question was an actual beauty queen. Her
name was Neha. In 2006 she won the title of Miss India, and represented our country in the Miss Universe pageant. She was a fashion model. She was trained in classical dance. I was back home
for Christmas in New Delhi, visiting friends and family. My cousin
and this beauty queen happened to have a friend in common. They
talked me up to her: *He's this great guy from America, he's an actor,
you should meet him.* For an entire week they tried to get her to
visit my parents' house—the same house I grew up in—but for one
reason or another, she could never make it.

Of course she can't make it, I thought. Miss Indias don't just
drop by and make house calls. But my cousin was persistent, and
eventually he arranged for the two of us to meet at the opening of
some bar.

What do you wear to meet a beauty queen? Well, I was going
through a phase I'll call "Dumpster Hollywood," which means torn

jeans that cost four hundred dollars, a jacket with a popped collar, an Ashton Kutcher trucker hat that said "Olé," a plaid scarf, and striped gloves with the fingers cut off.

Remember the movie *Who Framed Roger Rabbit*, when you first see Jessica in that red dress? That was my reaction when I first saw Neha. She was in fact wearing a red dress. At five foot ten she stood six foot three in heels, towering over my five-foot-eight pile of Dumpster Hollywood trash. (She would have been perfect for Dziko, I thought. Two giants.) She looked so stunning that I immediately assumed she would be a fake person. A plastic figurine. No one so beautiful could also be cool, smart, interesting. This is what we do to people when we're intimidated: we make them out to be monsters so we're more comfortable with ourselves. We judge. We demonize them to brace ourselves for rejection.

I introduced myself and we exchanged hellos.

Oh my God she's tall.

"Have a seat and I'll buy you a drink?" I suggested, thinking that if we were sitting down, I could level the playing field.

"Sure," she said. "I just have to say a quick hello to some other people, but I'll be back."

Sure she would.

I know that move. I've used it myself. The blow-off maneuver where you tell someone, "I'm just gonna run to the bathroom. I'll be right back," and you never see that person again. Your only contact is stalking them through Facebook.

"Hey," she said, smiling.

"Hey," I smoothly replied. "Have a seat." I rose ever so slightly, not wanting to expose my height again. I had found a corner table outside on the balcony where it was quiet. She sat down and pulled a cigarette from her purse.

I had bought us a couple of glasses of champagne and she took a sip. Her lips were glowing in the candlelight.*

"So you're an actor?" she asked.

"I'm on a TV show called *The Big Bang Theory.*"

"I've never heard of it."

Okay, so I can't play that card.

Instead we talked about our childhoods, growing up in New Delhi, discovered some friends we had in common. Gradually, I think she could tell I was not a creep (despite the trucker hat) and she began to open up. We chatted and chatted, and chatted some more. And then we really talked. "This is my first night out in almost a year," she said, looking away. At first I wasn't sure if her eyes were welling up with tears, or if the alcohol had begun to take hold. "I was engaged," she continued, "and two weeks before the wedding he called it off." She told me that the entire wedding had been planned. Tickets had been bought, venues had been selected, more than five hundred people had been invited, and then, just like that, it was all off. They were off. With her hands shaking ever so slightly, Neha pulled out another cigarette; I lifted the candle and lit it for her. "Cold feet," she said, almost to herself.

I broke the silence by making a joke about feet. Something about how I don't like them, and how my feet are whiter than Snow White's bottom. Maybe that sounds crass, given the circumstances, but I was trying to make her smile.

She explained to me that when it happened, at first she was in

---

* Helpful hint: Here's a cliché that happens to be true. Girls love it when you buy champagne.

shock, and then she was hugely embarrassed, mainly for her family, and how all her relatives still flew in to see her, because they had booked their tickets already. It was exactly like a wedding gathering, just without the main event. She told me that she had embarked on a spiritual path to try to make sense of the circumstances; she had embraced Buddhism, and it had saved her.

There was something beautiful about the rawness of her emotion, as if she had been to the very depths of heartache and survived, stronger, wiser, and more determined to find true love. Oh man, I had known her for two hours and I was getting hooked.

Finally it was time to say good night. She leaned in. "Do you want my number?"

"Nah, it's cool," I said. "I'll get it from someone else."

"Wouldn't it just be easier to take it now?"

"I'm good, I'll just get it from my cousin," I said, trying to be a baller. I was *really* trying to play it cool, but probably ended up looking like a dumbass jerk.

Thirty seconds after she left I called my cousin to get her number, and I immediately texted her to say I hope she made it home safe and that it was lovely chatting with her. As soon as I pressed SEND I kicked myself for seeming overeager; so much for being a baller.

Stupid stupid stupid—

She texted right back, saying she'd had a lovely night.

Later that night, my phone buzzed.

"I'm home safe. Thanks for being a gentleman."

❖

I didn't waste any time. In a few days I had to fly back to LA, and if I didn't do something, who knew when, or if, I'd see this goddess again? So the next morning I texted her and suggested we meet for dinner. She accepted. Quickly I tapped into my network of friends and cousins to find the best place to impress her, and we settled on a glitzy restaurant in the Oberoi hotel. My brother made a call to book the private glass wine room. I mean, she's *Miss India.* I had to bring out the big guns, right? I had to flash the big boys, right? I had to pull out all the stops, right? I had to bring my A-game, right? I'll stop; you get the point.

Once again I mused for hours over my fashion choices for the night. It was time to unleash the most expensive piece of clothing I have ever owned. (I mean, I had to whip out the big kahonas, right?) I picked a black wool sweater from Alexander Wang that goes all the way down to my knees. It looked like a woman's cape.

I arrived early to the restaurant, standing inside this small glass room and wearing my lady's cape. I knew there'd be a 50 percent chance she would think she had made a huge mistake, and then another 40 percent chance that she would confuse me for a woman. And a 10 percent chance that she wouldn't show.

Neha doesn't walk—she glides. I suppose she gets this from years of modeling. She glided (glode?) into the restaurant wearing all black, hair straight and flowing, and a hint of glitter on her face. She was a vision.

"Nice sweater," she said. I didn't know if she was being sincere or ironic.*

It was just a romantic dinner with Neha and me. Oh, and my brother, who wanted to meet her and invited himself into the glass room. Oh, and we had a fourth companion to our budding

---

* Fun fact: later, she did ask me if she could borrow "that pretty sweater" I'd worn on our first date.

romance: our waiter. As anyone who has ever eaten in a restaurant knows, typically, the waiter will swing by your table when needed, quickly refill your wine, and then leave you and your date in peace.

Not this guy. One "perk" of the private glass room is that he's *our private waiter*, which meant that he stood right next to us, always, his hands clasped behind his back like Ser Barristan, the Kingsguard from *Game of Thrones*. After some small chitchat my brother left us, but the Kingsguard remained, impassive, stoic, but inevitably hearing every word of our conversation.

When I told stories that made Neha laugh I peeked up at the Kingsguard, and when he didn't crack a smile I almost felt offended. I was speaking for two audiences—Neha and our waiter. He never did warm to me. She did.

It was a lovely date. Again we talked for hours. There was no licking of eyeballs; this just felt *real*, honest, right. Afterward we decided to have a nightcap at a bar full of middle-aged people dressed in tuxedos and gowns, dancing. I couldn't take my eyes off an elderly couple who slow-danced next to us, cheek to cheek. They looked so tender. So comfortable, so happy. I looked at that old couple and I thought, *Oh how lovely if that could be me and Neha one day.*

I turned to her and asked, "Tomorrow, do you want to meet my family?"

❖

Neha glided through the gate with a bouquet of flowers for my parents. They fell in love with her right away.

Neha is funny without *trying* to be funny. Some people tell stories at a party and work hard to make jokes. They're performing.

In the past, I had spent a lot of time with people in my industry—actors—and they usually tend to have a funny bone that's based on performance. It was refreshing to meet someone who didn't have that bone. Because there are two very different types of laughs:

1. The "Ha, that's clever" laugh.

2. The absolutely unconscious, laugh-out-loud, not-worried-what-you-sound-like laugh. That's the way I laughed when I met Neha. I genuinely found her funny, even when she wasn't making jokes. And to be honest, when she tries to make a joke she's terrible, which I find hilarious. One time at a lake we saw a couple of ducks fighting, and she said, "Look, the ducks are *beaking* each other up." Terrible or genius?

After dinner my mom said, "Kunal, why don't you bring up the guitar and sing Neha some songs?"

That's my mom: the world's best wingman. I brought out the trusty guitar and played "The Blower's Daughter" from Damien Rice. "*Can't take my eyes off yooooouu.*" Neha was impressed. Cha-ching!

One tiny problem, of course: my life was in Los Angeles, her life was in India.

"Do you want to pursue this further?" I asked her, finding a quiet moment after dinner.

She did.

"If we want this to go further, you will have to come to see me in LA. I'm filming and won't be able to come to India again till the summer."

Three weeks later she was on a flight to LA.

❖

At the time, I was living in a loft in LA, and for whatever trendy reason, the entire thing was a massive open space divided only by curtains. So on the off-off chance that in the next two weeks Neha needed to, say, use the toilet, I'd have to go hang out on the other side of the loft to give her privacy. Would the curtains freak her out? And what if she had weird body odor that I somehow hadn't noticed? Or what if she had weird feet? I'm not proud to admit this, but weird feet are pretty close to a deal breaker for me. Also, I should clarify that almost all feet are weird feet. Feet are gross. I used to date this girl who always wore open-toed sandals, and her feet were so stanky that when we climbed into bed I would casually suggest that she take a shower. The sound of people wearing flip-flops drives me batty, too. It's this unholy combination of sweaty arches and plastic and sun—puddles of sweat that smack the plastic in unison. *Smack, smack, smack.* Flip-flops should be banned.

Neha's plane was about to land. And truthfully, I actually hadn't seen her feet. We had kissed in New Delhi but nothing more. What imperfection would freak me out, and what imperfection of mine (I have plenty) would freak *her* out? There were so many unknowns.

Except I couldn't stop thinking, *I've met the woman I want to marry.*

My friends wouldn't need to wait long to meet her. Just a few hours after she arrived in LA, the entire cast of *The Big Bang Theory* was invited to go to dinner at the home of the president of Warner Bros. His dinner parties also included a movie screening, and we were subjected to Charlie Kaufman's film *Synecdoche, New York*, a four-hour art-house saga as difficult to watch as it is to pronounce. It's not exactly the perfect date film, especially after a twenty-two-hour flight.

So is this where the wheels came off? Is this where it all unraveled? Please. She's *Miss India*—she's used to being an ambassador of the country, and the woman carries herself with grace and class. More than that, though, she was *kind*. That's an underrated trait. Whenever a friend asks me for advice about someone they're dating, my first question to them isn't "Do they make you laugh?" (the usual question) but instead, "Are they kind?" When you're enamored with someone, you'll find them funny no matter what. But are they kind? How do they treat strangers? How do they speak to the doorman or the waiter?

I just *knew*. We didn't have a serious DTR (Define the Relationship) conversation where we formally established that we were boyfriend and girlfriend. We didn't need to clarify that we were monogamous. It just happened.

But what about that 8,490.62-mile distance between us? (I did the math.)

We had one simple tool: the phone. It doesn't get enough credit as a means of courtship.

We talked every day. Video chats? Facebook, Skype, Snapchat? Nope, they're the worst. When I saw her face on a computer screen, she became somehow *there but not really there*, and then I became shy, awkward, and instead of the deeper conversations, I'd cower behind small talk and self-conscious, nonsensical yammering. When I couldn't see her face, it freed us to speak openly and explore our innermost thoughts. We fell in love on the phone.

I don't think I would have found Neha if I hadn't been willing to risk failure. It would have been easy to play it safe and say that she was Out of My League, that we lived in different worlds and had too much ocean between us.

But you can't find love if you're not willing to lose it. You can't find happiness if you're not willing to risk being sad. And you can't find the love of your life without risking breaking your heart.

Dive in.

Puppies

RAISING A PUPPY MAKES ME NOT WANT TO HAVE CHILDREN. IS that bad? With babies, it's not even so much the constant waking up at night, or the free-floating anxiety that your kid has just eaten something forbidden, or that he will choke on one of his falling-out baby teeth. It's really just the all-consuming, aching fear that I'm not capable of taking care of someone who is absolutely dependent on me in every way. What if I fail? What if he does choke on a pebble? What if I forget to feed him and he starves to death? Or, honestly, how long will I have to continue picking up his monster shits?* Maybe that is the real reason why I don't want children: so that I don't have to touch another person's poop for the rest of my life.

---

* My dog shits like a monster. Not only the size of his poop, but the amount of times he goes. If I don't pick up his droppings from the backyard for, say, two days, I end up picking up sixteen shits. SIXTEEN SHITS. Do the math. On the bright side, how he nourishes the garden with his natural fertilizer.

My Big Fat Indian Wedding

MY WEDDING WAS JUST LIKE EVERY OTHER WEDDING. ONE thousand guests over a six-day period. There were people at my wedding that I didn't even know. Everyone was apparently my cousin. Strangers would pull me in for a hug and say, "Oh, you don't remember me? I was just a baby when you left India!"

We planned the whole thing in six months. We had to. Neha and I were engaged in June, and we wanted to get married in the winter in India. It's too hot in the summer, and instead of waiting for an entire year and a half, we decided on the coming December. Also when I say, "We planned the wedding," of course, like every groom, I mean "She planned the wedding." Neha went back to India for the entire six months and was the general of a wedding-planning army that included colonels like our parents, captains like our aunts and uncles and cousins, and countless hardworking lieutenants. (I didn't even make rank.) One of my older aunts was in charge of the flowers. A cousin was in charge of hotels. We had no wedding planner. What's the point? We had an army of a hundred and fifty family members standing by and ready to help in any way needed.

My job? Stay in America and serve as mediator between the

various parties involved. Which basically means that I had no idea what was going on.

After a day of shooting *Big Bang*, I would answer phone calls from Neha and from my mother, who would both say things like, "Your auntie isn't listening. What she doesn't grasp about the centerpieces is that—"

"Yes, Mom, I understand . . ." or "Yeah, I hear you, baby . . ." I would say, being as supportive as I could, and then drink myself to sleep.

Six months later it was time to hop onto the flight to India for my wedding week, and I really didn't have a clue what to expect. In some ways, I was just a guest at an incredibly elaborate family event.

Here we go.

DAY 1: ARRIVAL

When I landed in India and stepped up to the immigration line, I saw my brother *inside* the airport waving me over to the special diplomat line. He was somehow not only inside the airport but also *at the immigration desk*. He had convinced the officials to let me skip the line for immigration by waving around some special handwritten note from India's vice president (*apparently*). He also gave an emotional speech to the duty-free manager to allow us to buy more than our allotted quota of booze. "It's my brother's wedding, and he's got a rare terminal disease so this is our last time together. . . ." Once outside, balancing the copious bottles of scotch, I was greeted by Neha and twenty-five cousins (not an exaggeration), who gave me a pointy hat and sunglasses that said "Groom." They popped bottles of champagne, dousing me with the bubbles and lit firecrackers, right there in the airport parking lot.

"To the groom!!!!"

A little jet-lagged, buzzed from the champagne, and only a little worried that we might get arrested before the wedding, I drank in the experience and floated back to my family home, with Neha beside me. When we turned onto my street I could see a faint glow of illumination coming from the direction of the house, and as we grew closer I saw that the entire house was covered by a yellow and green and orange tent that looked like Cirque du Soleil, and a thousand shiny lightbulbs that hung from the balcony all the way to the ground. Everything smelled like flowers. Mom had prepared some butter chicken, we broke into the fourteen bottles of Scotch we had purchased at duty-free, and I realized that this massive homecoming—with lights and the food and my cousins and closest friends and Neha—was just a small taste of what was to come.

DAY 2: COCKTAIL PARTY

I woke up in a fog of jet lag to a loud, incessant clapping sound coming from the front door. It sounded like the opposite of applause, more like one of those toy monkeys with the cymbals that you wind up and they bang their hands together for hours. I staggered toward our front door and peeked outside. There I saw a crowd of eunuchs creating a ruckus. I hid behind a frosted windowpane and watched the scene unfold. In New Delhi, every neighborhood has a group of eunuchs called *hijra*s, who, according to tradition, show up before the wedding to bless the bride and groom. Except this "blessing" isn't exactly free; you have to *pay* them to go away, and if you refuse to give them cash, you not only don't get a blessing, they will plague your wedding with a curse. We had known this particular band of *hijra*s for years. They're friendly neighbors. It was a custom to get their blessing, and I didn't want to start the week with the *hijra* curse.

"Bring out the groom!" I heard them chanting.

"Shhhh! The groom is sleeping!" said a cousin, ever protective.

CLAP-CLAP-CLAP!

"Bring out the groom!"

"Come back later!" hissed my cousin.

CLAP-CLAP-CLAP!

Then I heard my mother negotiating a price for their blessing, and six hundred dollars later they did a little dance and gave their blessing for Neha and me. (Therefore, if anything bad were ever to happen between us, I'll blame the gang of neighborhood eunuchs.)

That crisis resolved, I shook off my jet lag and jumped into my actual responsibilities, which were to make sure that all my guests from America, about thirty-five of them, were taken care of, had hotels, and knew the basics of how to get around. India can be a shock to the senses. If you're a first-time visitor it's hard to process the number of people, the endless colors, the exotic smells—it really does feel like a different planet—so I wanted to be there to help everyone ease in.

I guided my guests to the first official function of the wedding, a small cocktail party at my parents' house. When I say "guided," I mean I told them to wash up, get over their jet lag, and get on the bus that would be waiting outside their hotel at exactly 8 p.m. It was like herding cats, if cats were your closest friends whom you'd invited to your wedding. The cocktail party was designed to be the calm before the storm. We only invited our inner family, closest friends, and guests from out of town. Three hundred people.

Neha looked gorgeous that night (and every night). She was dressed to the nines in a gold shirt, blue suede pants, and high heels—she looked like a goddess. I, on the other hand, looked like I hadn't slept in thirty-six hours, and I had one of those beneath-the-skin pimples that I covered with makeup. (Yes, MAKEUP. Get used to it.) Every time I hugged someone, I left a small makeup smear on the clothes of the hug recipient.

I witnessed the converging of all my worlds—a mix of childhood friends, adult friends, many, many cousins, aunts, uncles, and all my friends from America. I was so high in that moment. But it wasn't from the alcohol. I had drink after drink but I never felt drunk; instead I felt a *clarity* about how lucky I was to be with so many loved ones. Once the party dwindled down, around 3 a.m., and I had kissed Neha good night—as per custom, she was staying at her parents' house for the week—the house became peaceful and quiet. I sat with my dad and my brother at the dining table. It felt like the years of old. It felt like nothing had changed.

My father took a deep breath. "Isn't this wonderful? Look at this house. Feel the energy. Feel the joy."

I looked around the house. Old photographs of my grandparents, our first family trip to Paris, me in a ninja costume. I sat on my trusted old rickety chair. It had begun to feel the weight of my bum after thirty years of sitting in the same spot.

"This is a great moment for both our families," my dad said. "You are a great son to us, and it gives us pride and joy that you have found a great woman, and the two of you will make a great life and family. We are very proud of you."

I had known that he was happy *for me*, of course, but I hadn't thought about how it truly made *my parents* happy as well. Their hard work had paid off. In Indian culture, when you are a father or mother, there's real pressure from society to get your children to marry. It's something you think about from the day your child is born. Yes, my marriage to Neha was a culmination of my dream, but it was also a culmination of my parents' dream, too, in ways that I was now beginning to understand.

DAY 3: SANGEET

The next day we took things up a notch. On the agenda was the Sangeet. The word *Sangeet* translates to "song and dance," and it was a party thrown by my parents in a beautiful large banquet hall. *Six hundred* people. Neha's best friend, a fashion designer,* had crafted all these lovely clothes for me, and for this particular function I wore a maroon *sherwani*** and looked like a Persian prince. Though I felt like an Indian one.

As our friends began to enter this massive banquet hall, without any warning I had to take a legendary poop. It was one of those that just come out of nowhere. As the guests filed inside and expected to chitchat with the groom, I was stuck on the toilet for what seemed like an eternity. I now think all the excitement, anticipation, and anxiety were being released from me. After the epic battle in the toilet, I raced back to the hall.

"Welcome to the party, sir! Would you like some champagne?" one of the waiters asked me.

---

* Ladies and gentlemen, let's give a shout-out to Sid Tytler!

** A long coat with lots of embroidery that buttons up the front.

A lot of people accepted the champagne. My father had the idea of offering everyone a glass of champagne as soon as they arrived. Fun and festive, right? Yes. Except what he had forgotten is that when people start with champagne and then switch to liquor, they get real sloppy, real quick. So this soon became the Shitfaced Family Party. Things began to turn wild, and soon some of my cousins were insisting that the bartenders pass around shots to all the guests. The shot of choice, a "nuclear burn," was a hue of neon blue and green and tasted like vodka and sugar and the faintly chemical aftertaste of food coloring. They were being consumed by the hundreds, nay, the thousands.

"Time for the performance!" the DJ shouted. "Please come to the dance floor!"

The room exploded in cheers.

This was the climax of the Sangeet: our cousins would treat us to a dance that they had practiced, a routine that, theoretically, they'd been rehearsing for weeks. Our cousins performed a medley of eight Bollywood and Hollywood songs. They were truly bad. Neha and I choked back our laughter as they flailed about the stage. It was *The Full Monty* without the stripping. Still, of course, we were deeply touched and charmed by their efforts. It was all in good fun. Next, one of Neha's aunts wowed us with a beautiful traditional solo dance. She strutted her stuff with vigor as the entire crowd cheered her on. Suddenly she slipped and fell out of sight and the DJ scratched the music to a halt.

"Are you okay?" Neha cried as we all raced to the stage.

Her aunt jumped to her feet and sprang back to life. The music restarted with a bang and she finished the dance with even more gusto. I swear our elders are made of sterner stuff than we are.

We all burst into applause, and the DJ opened the dance floor to the entire crowd of six hundred. The room became an Indian nightclub, with friends and uncles and children and grandparents dancing in one sweaty mob. Even the guests at the food stations were pumping their fists and shaking their hips as they filled their plates.

At midnight, finally, I had time to eat something. I shoved my face full of butter chicken, kebabs, *daal,* and naan. As I devoured my late-night meal, I watched my brother calmly deal with the ballroom's managers. He was sorting out all the bills for the food and the booze, and I realized what I had known all along. *He's a rock.* Stoic and strong. Someday I hope to have that much gravitas. I mean he *is* the older one; I guess it's his job to be reliable.*

Later, as in not long before the sun came up, I collapsed onto my bed fully clothed.

DAY 4: THE MEHNDI

I woke up the next morning still in my Prince of Persia pajamas. I groggily stripped off my clothes and jumped straight into the shower. The long nights, the jet lag, and the alcohol were catching up with me. But there was no slowing down; we were only halfway there.

Mehndi is an ancient ceremony where the womenfolk of

---

* My mother always wanted a daughter but she was stuck with me, so maybe that's why I am the emotional, soft-spoken, delicate man that I am—she raised me like a daughter.

the wedding congregate to eat, drink, make merry—and, most important, to apply henna to their hands. It's basically a big henna party for women. Traditionally it's an all-girl affair, but in modern times the men come, too, and it's our job to feed the women while they're waiting for the henna on their hands to dry. The bride's henna is usually the most elaborate and Neha's took more than three hours, as four people simultaneously worked on her arms and legs. I'd never seen her look more beautiful—so happy, her skin radiating in the sun.

Neha's family had organized the event to create the atmosphere of a village marketplace, inviting a crowd of actual cooks, dancers, and bangle merchants. These weren't some out-of-work actors trying to re-create a village vibe; these were *actual villagers* from nearby towns. It gave my American friends a taste of real India. No DJ or colored vodka shots; this was the atmosphere of rural India. There was even a local tarot card reader, complete with a green parrot. The parrot's job was to pick a card from the deck and hand it to the tarot reader, who would in turn tell you your future.

My friend Jason was first in line. The parrot looked Jason in the eye, considered, and then walked over to the deck and picked a card with its beak.

The tarot reader looked at the card. "You picked the Card of Death. This is not good."

Jason laughed nervously.

Next up: Dziko.

The parrot looked at Dziko, thought carefully, and then picked another card.

"Card of Death," said the tarot reader. "This is not good."

Dziko smiled his baby smile, and then he ate the parrot. (Not really, but I thought he was going to.) That parrot was one sadistic son of a bitch, because he picked the Card of Death for half our wedding party.

The real highlight of the Mehndi, though, was the Bloody Marys. They were handcrafted by a village bartender famous for making the finest Bloody Marys in the world. His secret ingredient? Curry. Later, when the Mehndi was coming to an end, I decided to ride the private bus that we had hired to transport all my friends back to their hotel. It was a perfect sunny afternoon and we were all drunk from having consumed an average of seventeen Bloody Marys each.

From the back of the bus, someone started slowly singing, "I'm just a poor boy, nobody loves me. . . ."

"I'm just a poor boy, nobody loves me!" A few others joined in.

"Spare him his life from this monstrosity!" the group rose in unison.

The next thing I know we're all standing in this bus with the windows open, belting out "Bohemian Rhapsody" at the top of our lungs.

We could have been anywhere in the world. But we were in New Delhi, on a bus, experiencing unfiltered joy, a euphoric crescendo of friendship.

Hours later, once I had sobered up, we had one final tradition before the actual wedding ceremony: the family songs. Neha and I had said good-bye that afternoon after the Mehndi—I was not allowed to see her again until the wedding. That night, in our separate homes, all of us had our own versions of the family songs. On the groom's side, all my aunts came to my house and sang bawdy songs about love and sex, laced with innuendo about the first night of marriage.

Across town, however, the bride's family was having a very different tradition. When she wasn't traveling or staying overseas, Neha, like many Indian women, had lived in her parents' home most of her life. This is traditional. When she married me and moved in with me, it would be a heart-wrenching moment for her parents. It would be the good-bye I'd had with my family so many years ago. The songs that her aunts sang that night weren't naughty ballads about the first night of marriage. Their songs were about a child becoming a woman. They were songs about leaving home. They were songs of farewell.

After the singing, I called Neha to ask her if she was okay. That week we had so precious little time together. Even when we were together in public we weren't *together* together; we were yanked in twenty directions at once to chat with a cousin or a friend or pose for a camera or get ready for the next big event.

Tonight, we could enjoy the simple pleasure of a phone call, like we had so many times from LA to India.

"How's your stomach feeling?" she asked.

"Maybe that last Bloody Mary wasn't the best idea."

"Yeah, you're always good until you get past sixteen," she said with a giggle.

I told her about singing "Bohemian Rhapsody," we laughed about the Evil Parrot, and we tried to figure out whether so-and-so was actually a cousin or a wedding crasher.

I fell asleep with a smile on my face.

Tomorrow I would marry Neha.

DAY 5: THE WEDDING

The Big Day. I woke up early to prepare for a traditional ceremony in my house, where my immediate family would say prayers and give me a ritual cleansing.

The ceremony called for me to take off my shirt, and then my brother, cousins, and parents would gently dab my skin with a turmeric-based paste. Turmeric is an Indian spice that's used in almost all food, known to have healing powers that improve complexion.* It's an ancient ritual whose origins go back five thousand years.

I took off my shirt, self-conscious, feeling that I had packed on the pounds.

"At least you could have shaved your chest," said my brother.

Then my brother grabbed a handful of the paste, and instead of the gentle dabbing, he slathered it all over my face and hair and chest, laughing. The cousins soon joined in, covering me head to toe in turmeric, those wiseasses. The paste is yellow and sticky and feels like spicy honey. Suddenly we were all just kids again, running around chasing each other and screaming.

"Give me a hug!" I told my brother, and before he could dodge me, I managed to catch him and give him a bear hug, smearing him with the paste. He laughed, and gripped me tighter and pressed me closer. Normally, my brother isn't a hugger. But today he was saying a lot with this hug. We looked at each other, we squeezed again, and that was enough. No words were needed.

I jumped in the shower and cleansed myself of the cleansing, then stepped into my Wedding Day Outfit. Neha's fashion

---

* Where was this powder three days ago when I had my pimple?

friend had designed an outfit that, well, can only be described as something Liberace would have worn to his wedding. A golden velvet jacket with a flourish of peacock blue. Topped with a red turban.

"Kunal, nice prince outfit," said my uncle. (I'm still not sure if he meant Indian prince or the artist formerly known as Prince, but either way he had a point.)

Then I grabbed my sword. I didn't make many suggestions for the wedding, but this was nonnegotiable: I wanted to wear a sword. Like the kings of old. This would be Indian tradition meets *Lord of the Rings* meets *Teenage Mutant Ninja Turtles*—how could you *not* wear a sword, right?

I held up the sword and presented it to my best friend, Jason. I looked him in the eye and said, "This sword has been in my family for three hundred years."

"I understand," he said solemnly.

"When I'm not carrying the sword, I am trusting it to you."

"I am honored," Jason said, almost bowing his head.

"This is important."

He nodded, moved, and I could tell the moment meant a lot to him. We hugged.

Little did he know that my parents had rented the sword for three dollars from the local antique shop. I grabbed my ceremonial sword and turban, marched from the house like a prince, and prepared to saddle my horse.

Horse? Yep. It's tradition for the groom to gallantly enter his wedding on a horse. Except we had two complications:

1. The wedding was forty miles away.
2. I'm scared of horses.

The first problem was an easy enough fix. I would mount this horse (more like a pony) next to my home, heroically pose for the photos, trot the horse to the end of the block, dismount the pony, get in a car, drive forty miles, and then, two blocks from the wedding venue, once again mount the horse (okay, pony) and ride into the wedding.*

As for my fear of horses? It was made even worse because the guy handling this horse, a fourteen-year-old kid, refused to feed the horse until he received payment. So the hungry horse was freaking the frack out. So I'm starting to freak the frack out.

"Don't you have any manners?!" my uncle roared at the kid, who still refused to back down.

I stared at this horse, which is angrily stomping its hooves and bucking its head, and I visualized my tombstone: KUNAL NAYYAR, DEAD ON HIS WEDDING DAY AFTER FALL FROM HUNGRY HORSE.

My dad came over to smooth things out, as always, and took care of the payment and the kid fed the horse.

I don't have fond memories of horses. Years ago I had taken one riding lesson, and the lesson ended when I fell off the horse. That was it. No riding ever again. Except this day. We trotted down one block, which felt like a hundred miles; somehow I didn't fall, and mercifully I climbed down from that awful beast. Then I hopped in the car with my brother and father and continued on to the wedding venue.

Halfway to the wedding I realized something. "I need to take a leak."

---

* I never did understand how the horse beat us to the venue. Maybe there were two horses. Or maybe it galloped really, really fast. Or maybe they transported the horse in a trailer. Or maybe no one cares.

"Can it wait?" asked my father.

"I'm stressed, Dad. I have no control over my bladder."

So the driver pulled over to the side of the road and—right there in public—I unzipped my fly and whipped it out.

"I need to pee, too," my father said.

"Me, too," said the driver.

"Yeah, what the hell," said my brother.

So the four of us, side by side, pulled down our pants and took a huge group pee.

Ahhhhhh!

Game on.

I had survived the horse, I had been cleansed, I had been relieved of pee, and now it was just butterflies and a marriage.

When we approached the wedding venue, the driver pulled over and I emerged from the car to find another white horse waiting to take me inside. *WTF, is it the same horse? Did the horse gallop its way over here? Is it faster than cars?**

Now full of adrenaline, I hopped on that pony. Flanked by my father and brother and friends, my sword at my side and feeling, indeed, like a king, I entered my wedding at last.

❖

At the start of the ceremony, there's a lovely tradition, called Milni, that matches up the men from both sides of the family. The name of my oldest uncle would be called out, then the name of Neha's oldest uncle, then the uncles would meet in the aisle, and then they would give each other flowers and a hug. Amid this embrace they would jovially try to pick the other off the ground. Not liter-

---

* Turns out it was my original horse's twin sister.

ally; this wasn't a competition of strength, just a ritual that represented the joining of two families. Cousins were matched with cousins, brothers with brothers.

It was a cold night. The wedding was outdoors. Purple flowers coated the ground and the walls and the tables, illuminated by soft purple lighting. It looked like a fantasy. My family escorted me to a little stage with two beautiful chairs. I sat in my chair and waited for Neha and for the first time all week I thought, *HOLY SHIT THIS IS HAPPENING*. Then, over the speakers a beautiful old Hindi hymn began to play, a religious hymn, and this announced the moment of Kanya Aagman: Neha's entrance.

She glided in as her brothers and cousins covered her with a blanket of flowers. I glimpsed her from afar . . . and could see that she was grinning. She didn't enter as some demure angel. She didn't pretend to be anything. She simply had the biggest smile on her face, joyous, soaking in every moment.

I couldn't believe that this woman was going to be my wife. I had never felt like this. Ever. Not with Grace. Not when I had other relationships that felt "real." There's real and there's REAL. This wasn't just a case of butterflies. This wasn't just a rapid beating heart. This was every single cell in my body singing.

Soon the priest was speaking in Sanskrit. We sat on our chairs, and I tried to understand him, but really, honestly, I couldn't understand a word. In fact, I was practically destroying the entire ceremony. At one point, for example, I was supposed to take this oil and throw it over my shoulder, but instead I took the oil and almost drank it, before the priest quickly stopped me from poisoning myself.

We stood up and walked seven steps around the fire, in what's known as the Saptapadi, and then we sat back down.

Then the priest kept saying more and more words.

"Kunal," Neha whispered. "We're married."

"We're married?"

Awesome! I had no idea.

❖

After the ceremony, at the receiving line, we posed for a photograph, then another, then another, and then a hundred, and then two hundred . . . and then, in total, five hundred photographs. Thank God Neha is a trained model and has that kind of stamina, because I was ready to kill myself. We stood there so long, in fact, that by the time the five hundredth person greeted us, the first greeter had already eaten dinner and danced and gone home. People were leaving and we hadn't finished posing.

We have one final tradition. It's called the Bidaai. When the dust settled and it was time for us to go home, Neha's parents would walk her from the wedding venue, arm in arm for the last time. Her final good-bye as their daughter, for now she was entering into a new family. This is a very sad moment in Indian weddings. Once she was in our car with me, all of her cousins and brothers would get behind the car and push us for a few moments as we began our journey home.

Neha slowly walked to my car with her father, and she began to cry. Her parents began to cry. And by now, dear reader, you've read enough of this book to know that I started crying, too.

"Stop crying, you idiot," my brother whispered to me.

"It's a sad moment," I said.

"For them! Not for you! You're bringing her to our house!"

I tried to wipe away the tears.

"They'll think you're not happy to bring her home. What's wrong with you?" my brother said, incredulous.

We got in the car. Neha's brothers stood behind us and began to push the car. The engine kicked into gear and we were on our way.

She looked at me, I looked at her, and then I drove home.

With my wife.

DAY 6: THE RECEPTION

The next morning I had that schoolboy feeling again. *My wife!* We had more people over that morning (of course we did), and following an old tradition, the bride "showed her face" to all my friends and family. (This harks back to the olden times, when you wouldn't have seen the face of the woman you'd married until it was too late. Suckers.) Now it's purely ceremonial. Neha put a shawl over her face, then I lifted it and theatrically proclaimed, "*This* is my *wife!*"

As the shawl lifted she crossed her eyes and stuck out her tongue, then started making monster noises. The family ate it up.

My wife.

The night after the wedding, we had a reception for a thousand people, we hugged more cousins (or were some of them wedding crashers?), we drank more champagne, and we said farewell to our guests. We followed more customs and embraced more traditions—describing them all would take another seventy pages. And truthfully I myself don't remember much of the reception. I was lost in thought. I couldn't soak up any more emotion. I felt so lucky to have been raised in this culture. I love America and I love living in Los Angeles, but in growing up here I was blessed with so much joy, and I felt such a sense of *rightness* when I fully immersed myself in everything that came with our wedding. The customs are about family. Love. Life. I was proud to be Indian. I *am* proud to be Indian.

The week reminded me that nothing is unachievable when you have the support of your family. We planned a one-thousand-person wedding in six months. In fact, come to think of it, we planned a second wedding, too.

Soon after landing back in America, we arranged an official courthouse wedding at a city court in Beverly Hills, mostly for legal reasons. We invited two guests: my friends Tim and Jason. (This time Jason didn't have to carry my sword.) I wore a suit and Neha wore a cute dress.

A beautiful, tall, African-American woman with big curly hair and large diamonds led us through our vows, and as she spoke, I realized that her words had the same cadence, the same themes, and the same core message as the ones said by our Indian priest. She talked about love. About family, and about what it means to be a husband and wife.

So much is different in these two cultures. And so much is exactly the same.

In other words, as I said in the beginning . . .

My wedding was just like every other wedding.

Holiday Traditions Part 4: Diwali

Diwali (*De-WALL-ee*) *n.* An ancient Hindu festival
celebrated in autumn every year, considered
India's New Year and the Festival of Lights.

THE FESTIVAL OF LIGHTS SIGNIFIES THE HINDU NEW YEAR,
and celebrates that Lord Rama, after defeating the evil king Ravana (remember them from page 74?), has finally come back to his
kingdom. When Lord Rama returned after fourteen years of exile
(think: Aragorn), the ancient city of Ayodhya illuminated the entire kingdom with *diya*s (oil lamps) to show respect and gratitude
for their beloved king.

This is my favorite Indian festival because every house in India
is lit up with *diya*s and candles, every balcony, wall, and roof shim-
mering with a brilliant hue of fiery yellow. On Diwali, the entire
country is literally glowing. It's like Christmas lights without the
electricity.

A big part of the tradition is that you give your house a deep
cleaning, scrubbing every nook and cranny. Once your home is
cleansed, you leave every door and window open to invite Lakshmi,
the goddess of wealth, to come and bless your home.

The biggest part of Diwali is the fireworks. Tons and tons of

fireworks. And I don't mean fireworks like big firework displays
with all these safety regulations. I mean fireworks in your home,
in your driveway, exploded by your own two hands! Fireworks are
legal in India so we just jump the gun and start exploding them a
few days early. It's always open season. As kids we threw fireworks
at each other;* we hid fireworks in each other's bags so they would
get discovered by the principal. Occasionally, because some of the
fireworks were so cheap and poorly made, they would just explode
in your face of their own accord.

Diwali is also a very spiritual night, because it signifies the beginning of our new year. Every Diwali, my family huddled into my
grandfather's old office, and we recited a prayer called the Gayatri
Mantra seven times. (The prayer is roughly the equivalent of Chris-
tianity's Lord's Prayer.)

My grandfather's office was a special place to us. He had been
a prominent dentist, and, in fact, he had been the personal dentist
to the president of India. My grandfather had a clinic in our house,
and he kept his practice going until the day he died. Even months
after his death, patients would come to our house and hope to see
him for an appointment. My grandfather used the office to hand-
craft the tooth caps, braces, and dentures that he provided to his
patients. So we left the office intact as a tribute to him, and that's
where we'd stand shoulder-to-shoulder, reciting the Gayatri Mantra in his honor.

Now, in my own home in Los Angeles, one that came with walls
instead of flowing white curtains, I keep Diwali alive. My wife and
I light the entire house with candles. My American friends who at-
tended my wedding in India still have all of their traditional Indian

---

* Note: Don't try this at home. This means you!

clothes, so we all dress up and eat Indian food, clean the house, and leave the doors open so the goddess of wealth can come and grace our home. We built a small Hindu temple to honor our family and our grandparents. And every year, in that small temple, my wife and I say the Gayatri Mantra seven times.

Diwali (*De-WALL-ee*) *n.* 1. An ancient Hindu festival celebrated in autumn every year, considered India's New Year and the Festival of Lights. 2. A perfect opportunity to remember where you come from, to honor where you are, and to keep traditions alive for the future.

Good-bye

I'VE NEVER BEEN GOOD WITH GOOD-BYES. I HAVE HAD TO say a lot of good-byes in my life. It never gets easier. Even writing these words is hard.

When I set out to write this book I didn't know it was going to be a soppy joyride of heartbreak, failure, culture shock, and triumph. I just wanted to share my story because I thought maybe it would help people believe that *anything* is possible. And it is.

Adieu my dear reader,
I will miss you more than you know.

A Thought Recorded on an
Aeroplane Cocktail Napkin

Every now and then, make a list of some things you know for sure; share them with the world.

Acknowledgments

HERE ARE SOME OF THE PEOPLE RESPONSIBLE FOR ALL THE love, heartache, inspiration, and laughter that make up this book— in no particular order, I think.

Chris, Ben, JR. Sarah. Chance, Morgan, James, Michael, Corey, Arnica, and Jenny. Shact, Bitner & Diaby.

Jim Stein, Matt Shaffer, Jonathan Howard, and the entire Innovative family. Scott Harris for dancing at my wedding.

Steve Lovett for your never-say-never attitude.

Kaley, Jim, Johnny, Simon, Melissa, and Mayim, for being my family away from home.

Mark Cendrowski, Nikki Lorre, Anthony Rich, and the entire *Big Bang* crew for proving that miracles do come true if we stick together.

Bill, Steve, Chuck, and all the writers on *Big Bang* who inspire me to be a better writer every day.

Chuck Lorre, for giving me the opportunity of a lifetime and teaching me the true meaning of humility and hard work.

Rob Weisbach, for gently pushing me every day to finish this book—I cried, I fought, I had anxiety attacks, and all the while you encouraged me to keep going. You made me believe in myself. Thank you also for keeping my acid reflux at bay.

Peter Borland and the entire Simon & Schuster team, for not only believing in me but also providing me with pages to write upon. You gave me a platform from which I could share my story. I am forever in your debt.

Jeff Wilser, for listening to stories from my whole life, and then actually going to India and experiencing it for yourself. You are a champion, sir. Let's do one more!

Anmol Nayyar. I have always wanted to be like you. You embody honesty, strength, and poise. I hope you like this book; your blessing means everything to me. I am lucky to be your little brother.

Rama Mom and Gulshan Dad. Thank you for your support, encouragement, and acceptance of my family and me. And for throwing one hell of a wedding!

To the Nayyars, Grewals, Bawas, Dhawans, Kapurs, Bhandaris, and all the rest of my family not mentioned here (mainly because it would take an entire other book), I thank you all for being my security blanket.

Manavi. Cousin Shmuzin—you're my real sister and you know it. Thank you for being my biggest champion.

Dad. Everything I have to say is in the book. You're the reason these pages exist.

Jason. There is not one person I trust more with my career than you. Thank you for proving that brothers don't always have to come from the same mother. Also, thank you for introducing me to sushi and golf.

Neha. Thank you for not divorcing me when I was spending

more time on my laptop than in the bedroom. You're the real prize. Everything compared to you is second best.

And finally, to you, dear reader, for spending your hard-earned money on this book. I owe so much to you. Thank you for joining me on this ride.